THE
FIVE-FOLD PRAYER

THE FIVE-FOLD PRAYER

A HOLY SPIRIT INSPIRED PRAYER MODEL THAT ENSURES 100 % ANSWERS TO ALL YOUR PRAYERS

DR. JEFFREY W. VAN WYK

THE FIVE-FOLD PRAYER

© 2010 Dr. Jeffrey W. van Wyk

ISBN 978-1-456-40531-1

This book is designed to provide condensed information. It is not intended to reprint all the information that is otherwise available, but instead to complement, amplify and supplement other texts. You are urged to read all the available material, learn as much as possible and tailor the information to your individual needs. Every effort has been made to make this book as complete and as accurate as possible. However, there may be mistakes, both typographical and in content. Therefore, this text should be used only as a general guide and not as the ultimate source of information. The author shall have neither liability nor responsibility to any person or entity with respect to any loss or damage caused, or alleged to have been caused, directly or indirectly, by the information contained in this book.

All rights reserved. No part of this publication may be reproduced, stored in or introduced into a retrieval system, or transmitted, in any form, or by any means (electronic, mechanical, photocopying, recording or otherwise) without the prior written permission of the publisher. Any person who does any unauthorized act in relation to this publication may be liable to criminal prosecution and civil claims for damages.

Published by:

All Scripture quotations, unless otherwise indicated, are taken from the New King James Version of the Bible. Copyright © 1982 by Thomas Nelson, Inc. Used by permission. All rights reserved.

I dedicate this book to my wife, Marlene, who has stood faithfully with me in ministry. Without her constant prayers and loving support, I would not have been able to achieve success in ministry.

Contents

Introduction	1
1. Effective Fervent Prayer	13
2. All Kinds of Prayer	31
3. The Prayer Life of Jesus	55
4. Fasting	73
5. A New Prayer Language	89
6. Prayer, Praise and Worship	117
7. Examples of a Prayer Book	125
8. Prayer References from the Word	145

Introduction

Definition of prayer

Prayer is simply communication with God. This can be through spoken words, written words, tongues, meditation, or song.

God desires us to talk to Him and prayer is one way of doing so. Prayer is not for us to selfishly ask God for things, but to honor and glorify God by spending time with Him.

Prayer is a command of God and is to be practiced both in public and in private. Such a command brings those that have the spirit of prayer into great intimacy with God. Prayer will ensure great things from God, both for the person that prayed and for those who are prayed for.

Many people think of prayer as being a one way communication. Yet prayer can and should be both ways, with us also listening to what God has to say. God can speak to us through the Bible, through others, through circumstances, but especially through His Holy Spirit. God can place specific words and thoughts in our minds and even speak to us in an audible voice.

Through prayer we actually experience relationship with God. The quality of our prayer life determines the quality of our relationship with God. Prayer is talking with God. Prayer is listening to God. Prayer is enjoying the presence of God.

Prayer can take many forms such as worship, confession, thanksgiving, praising, asking for things, waiting silently and listening.

Prayer is not simply saying words. It is not repeating formulas. God is looking for a heartfelt relationship.

We pray because we love God. We spend time with God in prayer and communion because we love Him. Just as a man and woman in love desire to be together and communicate, so we desire to be with Him and to fellowship with Him in proportion to our love for Him.

We pray because we depend on God. God is our source. Through prayer we receive the comfort, the strength and all the other resources that we need in life both naturally and spiritually.

We need to pray because God commands us to pray.

> Colossians 4:2
> Continue earnestly in prayer, being vigilant in it with thanksgiving.

Jesus prayed constantly and was always in perfect communion with the Father. He always knew what the Father wanted, what the Father was saying, and what the Father was doing.

INTRODUCTION

The call to prayer

> 2 Chronicles 7:14
> If My people who are called by My name will humble themselves, and pray and seek My face, and turn from their wicked ways, then I will hear from heaven, and will forgive their sin and heal their land.

God's people have a responsibility to acknowledge their sins and repent. If we want to be reconciled to God we need to be in right standing with Him.

In the above context, God is speaking only to His people. That places an enormous responsibility on believers as they carry the seed of healing for their entire nation.

When unbelievers see disasters come upon them they can cry out and want God to hear them. But unlike true believers they have no assurance that God will hear them. Clearly this promise does not belong to them.

Promises are the backbone of the believer and shape the whole character of the church. God's promises reveal the way He has promised to work with His people. Through Jesus Christ we now know on what basis God can forgive His people their sins.

This promise applies to present day believers and if we follow these instructions we can release a spiritual revival in the church and in our nation.

The prerequisites are:

- We need to be a people who are called by His name
- We need to humble ourselves
- We need to pray
- We need to seek His face
- We need to turn from our wicked ways

All these steps are necessary and can only happen in this order.

Be bold

> Hebrews 4:16
> Let us therefore come boldly to the throne of grace that we may obtain mercy and find grace to help in time of need.

This passage of Scripture is a priestly expression used in the Old Testament for priests in their approach to God. Only certain people had this privilege. But now we who are in Christ can all draw near to God in worship and prayer.

All believers have the priestly privilege of access to God. This can be done boldly without fear or rejection. We have freedom to approach God without hesitation or inhibition because of the blood of Jesus.

Have a secure place to pray

> Matthew 6:6
>
> But you, when you pray, go into your room, and when you have shut your door, pray to your Father who is in the secret place; and your Father who sees in secret will reward you openly.

Make sure you have a place to go where you can pray in private without any hindrances or interruptions. Christians who do not have a prayer room usually do not pray. I once moved from a large house to a very tiny one. The result was that I had no private place to go for my prayer time and my prayer life suffered. This caused me to grow lukewarm towards God and as a result my finances began to suffer.

Also make sure there are no distractions like cell phones, etc. Having worship music playing in the background sets a very good atmosphere for prayer. Also make sure that you do not go into your prayer room without your Bible because it is the living seed of God.

Build a structured prayer life

> Matthew 6:7
>
> And when you pray, do not use vain repetitions as the heathen do. For they think that they will be heard for their many words.

THE FIVE-FOLD PRAYER

It is important to take a structured prayer plan with you when you pray. This is suggested for the following reasons:

- To ensure that you avoid vain repetitions when praying
- To ensure that you include everyone and everything when you pray
- To ensure that your prayer time is consistent and effective
- To keep a record of prayer requests

Include a prayer structure with all the relevant passages of Scriptures in a prayer book. Write down your prayer requests in your book and make sure you write in the dates as well. Have a column where you can record the date that prayer was answered.

I also have all my prophecies written down in my prayer book which reminds me of God's promises, plans and purposes for my life. I also include all the written petitions which I have made to the Lord.

There are certain prayers and related passages of Scripture which I read out from my prayer book. This may sound very religious or formal, but our memory fails us and we need to bring all our needs to the Lord in prayer by making detailed declarations and petitions.

INTRODUCTION

Have a purpose

Have a purpose in prayer. Know what you are going to pray about. It is difficult to pray fervently without knowing what you want or desire from God. We should have a clear cut well defined idea about what we are asking God for. If you do not have this, wait on God until He reveals His purpose for your prayer time.

Postures of prayer

Some Christians believe that all prayers in church should be offered on our knees. According to Scripture, prayers are presented to God by His people in different circumstances and physical postures.

a. Kneeling

There are many examples of people praying to the Lord on their knees, suggesting that this was a common practice. Daniel prayed on his knees three times a day. Peter knelt down before the corpse of Tabitha to pray for her before she came back to life. Kneeling was a ritual expression of the willing surrender of the life of the worshipper to God.

b. Standing

Standing before the Lord in prayer was also a common practice, perhaps more common than kneeling. One of the most impressive cases is when Jehoshaphat invited the people to pray. He stood up in the assembly in the house of the Lord and prayed for liberation while the people stood before the Lord.

The Jews used to pray standing in the synagogues and on the street corners to display their piety.

Standing in prayer emphasizes the freedom we have to approach God.

c. Sitting down

The practice of praying while sitting down is rare in the Bible but not entirely absent. King David sat before the Lord and prayed.

This is the posture assumed by individual seeking instructions from the Lord or through His prophet.

d. Lying down on the bed

We also find in the Bible cases in which people prayed during the night while lying on their beds and meditated on Him. This posture provides an opportunity to meditate on the goodness of the Lord while seeking His help.

e. Prostrate

In religious contexts this is a posture of worship. It is fundamentally an expression of homage and submission before a superior.

When prostrating, people place their full body horizontally on the ground with their face on the floor usually with outstretched arms. There are many cases in the Bible where people lay prostrate before God.

This brief review indicates that Biblically there was not a particular posture in which worshippers were required to pray. Postures are important only to the extent that they are the external expression of reverence, inner feelings, and commitments to the Lord. Any attempt to select one as superior and indispensable over the others lacks Biblical support.

Words are powerful

There is a contest in the heavenly realm for your words. Your mouth will employ either Satan and his power or God and His power. Your words will either employ the cycle of death or the cycle of life.

> Joshua 1:8
> This book of the law shall not depart out of your mouth; but you shall meditate therein day and night, that may observe to do according to all that is written therein: for

then you shall make your way prosperous, and then you shall have good success.

Read the book of Joshua and discover how successful he was.

Mark 11:23
For I say to you, that whosoever shall say to this mountain, "Be removed, and be cast into the sea" and shall not doubt in his heart, but shall believe that those things which he says shall come to pass; he shall have whatsoever he says.

Thanksgiving

It is good to begin your prayer with thanksgiving and praise.

Psalm 100:4
Enter into His gates with thanksgiving, and into His courts with praise. Be thankful to Him, and bless His name.

Thank God for answers to prayer and tell Him how great He is. Use the Word of God to praise God.

Thanking God will increase your faith. Praising God will also increase your faith because you will begin to fix your eyes on God and His faithfulness and not on your problem.

INTRODUCTION

The names of God

When you structure your prayers, include the names of God as they manifest and declare His abilities to supply all your needs.

Remember, Jesus is Jehovah and He revealed himself as such in the Old Testament as well as in the New Testament.

Jehovah Elohim	Creator God
Jehovah El Shaddai	Almighty God
Jehovah Jirah	The Lord is my Provider
Jehovah Rapha	The Lord is my Healer
Jehovah Nissi	The Lord is my Champion
Jehovah Shalom	The Lord is my Peace
Jehovah Rohi	The Lord is my Shepherd
Jehovah Tsidkenu	The Lord is my Righteousness
Jehovah Mkeddesh	The Lord is my Sanctification
Jehovah Shammah	The Lord is my Ever Present God

THE FIVE-FOLD PRAYER

How is prayer answered?

The Bible reveals that prayer is answered:

- Immediately at times: Isaiah 65:24; Daniel 9:21-23
- Delayed at times: Luke 18:7
- Different from our desires: 2 Corinthians 12:8-9
- Beyond our expectations: Jeremiah 33:3; Ephesians 3:20

Just a thought....

There is a price to pay for the manifest presence of God that will release miracles, signs and wonders that can transform our communities with the power of God's Spirit. None of this can be a reality without praying and spending time in the presence of God. We are living in a dying world and the church will only come to life again when it discovers the vital reality of radical sacrificial prayer. Someone once said "A church is never more like the New Testament church than when it is praying."

CHAPTER 1

Effective Fervent Prayer

> James 5:16
> The effective, fervent prayer of a righteous man avails much.

This is a powerful passage of Scripture on prayer. It promises that if certain conditions are met, we have the assurance that all our prayers will be answered. 100% answered prayer! What a wonderful promise God gives to His children who learn to prayer effectively in accordance with His Word.

Do you believe that God can and will answer every one of your prayers? Many of God's people pray, but in their hearts they do not really believe that God will come through for them. Can you remember the story in Acts where the church was praying for Peter when he was thrown into prison? God heard them and answered their prayer and Peter was released. He arrived at the door of the gate and knocked. When they were told that Peter was free and at the gate, they did not believe it and continued praying.

James gives us an indication of what fervent effective prayers can produce.

> James 5:17
>
> Elijah was a man with a nature like ours, and he prayed earnestly that it would not rain; and it did not rain on the land for three years and six months.

God has provided us with a supernatural resource that can effectively and positively shape our future and destiny.

Just believing produces nothing

Many walk around and say "I believe I believe". Well, just believing will not bring in your harvest. It is like a farmer walking in his fields and saying "I believe I am going to reap a harvest." But he will reap nothing unless he places seed into the ground first. He must take his bag of seed into the field and plant that seed into the ground. He must then wait patiently for his harvest.

Be persistent

> Luke 18:1-8
>
> And there was a widow in that city; and she came unto him, saying, "Avenge me of my adversary." And he would not for a while: but afterward he said within himself, "Though I fear not God, nor regard man; Yet because this widow troubles me, I will avenge her, lest by her continual coming she weary me." And shall not God avenge His own elect, which cry day and night unto him, though He bear long with them?

Impatience is short sighted. God answers prayer in His timing, in His way, and for His purpose. Although we may not understand why, perseverance may bring unexpected blessings.

Praying will take persistence and diligence. We must be devoted to prayer, applying ourselves to it with much diligence. The Spirit of God will enable us with the strength and power needed to make the prayer effective.

Jesus wants us to be persistent with our prayers. It is not a matter of wearing God out with our prayers but by praying persistently we are proving that our faith is genuine.

If every prayer we prayed was answered immediately, we would not have to exercise any faith. Jesus said that we should always pray and not give up. He would never have told us that if our prayers were not going to be answered. He has promised that if we pray persistently our prayers will be answered, even beyond all we can ask or imagine.

Forgive others

> Mark 11:25
> And when you stand praying, forgive, if you have ought against any: that your Father also which is in heaven may forgive you your trespasses.

We cannot dare go before God and ask him to forgive us if we refuse to forgive others. God's grace is to be shared and if we do not share that grace we lose its blessing. We are forgiven so that we can be agents of forgiveness.

Unforgiveness is something that can really hold us back from escaping the corruption of sin and living for God. Unforgiveness comes in many forms, such as bitterness, hatred, malice, holding grudges, and resentment. It can actually block God from forgiving our sin and provide a foothold for the devil to influence our lives.

God expects us to forgive others just as He has forgiven us. God is perfect and sacrificed his Son Jesus so that our sin penalty would be paid. Because of our faith in Christ, God forgives us from our sin. If we refuse to forgive another person for an offense we are dishonoring the forgiveness that God gave us. God will hold us accountable for this.

Just as God has forgiven us we need to forgive ourselves for our sin as well. When we release ourselves from this self-judgment we will become the new person that God intends us to be.

Pray without ceasing

> 1 Thessalonians 5:17
> Pray without ceasing.

How does one pray continually? We cannot always be on our knees. With the daily demands on our busy lives we are not able to be in constant prayer.

Maintaining a healthy relationship requires communication. Effective prayer is a proper heart attitude and expresses itself throughout the day with silent prayers of communication and agreement with the Lord.

When we are in agreement with the Spirit we are praying continuously. The heart attitude of praying without ceasing means an ever open heart to the Lord's leading.

We can be open to the leading of the Spirit when He urges us to pray for something or someone. At that time we can agree with God and make a mental note to add that concern to our later prayer time.

Praying without ceasing does not take the place of time alone in prayer with God but it is being open to the leading of the Lord who lays burdens on our hearts at any time of the day or night.

Pray in the Holy Spirit

> 1 Corinthians 14:2
> But he who speaks in a tongue does not speak to men but to God, for no-one understands him; however, in the spirit he speaks mysteries.

Another way to ensure an effective prayer life is to pray in the Holy Spirit. To pray in the Holy Spirit means to pray in tongues.

We are commanded to spend time praying with the Spirit.

> 1 Corinthians 14:14-15
>
> For if I pray in a tongue, my spirit prays, but my understanding is unfruitful. What is the conclusion then? I will pray with the spirit...

Pray the Word

We should pray in accordance with the Word of God.

> Hebrews 4:12
>
> For the word of God is living and powerful and sharper than any two-edged sword, piercing even to the division of soul and spirit, and of joints and marrow, and is a discerner of the thoughts and intents of the heart.

Prayer that brings results must be based on the Word of God. God's Word is a seed that produces a harvest when sown.

> Ephesians 4:29
>
> Let no corrupt word proceed out of your mouth, but what is good for necessary edification, that it may impart grace to the hearers.

When God's incorruptible word is spoken in any situation it brings forth results and accomplishes that for which it is spoken.

So pray the Word of God and succeed. Be an overcomer and move forward in victory over any and every situation that may face you. Your success depends on what you have to say and not what the devil has to say.

Prayer and speaking the Word of God go hand in hand. When you quote the Word of God on any issue you are praying the most powerful prayer ever prayed. The Word of God has the power to make things happen. Nothing just happens. Something must be set in motion whether in the natural or in the Spirit realm.

When God's Word is spoken out in the natural it has an effect on the Spirit realm. Praying God's Word is saying to God what God has already said.

> Isaiah 55:11
> So shall my word be that goes forth out of my mouth: it shall not return unto me void, but it shall accomplish that which I please, and it shall prosper in the thing whereto I sent it.

For example, God sent Word for healing. Find out what that Word is. Put that same Word in your mouth and send it back to God. God says His Word shall not return to Him void or useless and if it that is true, what is the return? It has to be healing. That is the harvest. That is the physical manifestation of praying God's Word over sickness.

Now use that kind of prayer by praying God's living Word in any situation you may find yourself. Apply it to your marriage, your finances, your career, your ministry or any need you may have. God has the answer in His Word.

Prayers of confession

> Proverbs 28:13
> He who conceals his transgressions will not prosper, but he who confesses and forsakes them will find compassion.

> James 5:16
> Confess your trespasses to one another, and pray for one another, that you may be healed. The effective, fervent prayer of a righteous man avails much.

Confession breaks the power of the devil. Proclaiming something out loud to others carries incredible power whether it is marriage vows, declarations of faith, or confessions. There is something powerful about exposing hidden things to the light. This is particularly true when it comes to confession.

Sin which has not been confessed hardens our hearts. The Bible warns us to protect our hearts.

Putting the specific sin into words is necessary because words carry power.

Sin gives ground to Satan and allows him into our lives, our minds and our hearts. The burden of sin is a heavy one that grows heavier over time and weighs us down in all aspects of our life. Allow prayers of confession to help lighten your burden and the burden of others.

Follow these steps:

- Recognize and put the sin into words
- Repent and turn away from that sin
- Renounce any level of demonic activity that has occurred as a result of the sin
- Ask to be forgiven

Ask

> 1 John 5:14
> Now this is the confidence that we have in Him, that if we ask anything according to His will, He hears us.

Why should we pray if God already knows what we need before we ask?

Prayer was not intended to inform God of something He does not already know. Prayer is not merely to receive what we want but to nurture our relationship with God. As a result, prayer can change us rather than the situation, reinforcing our confidence in God and realigning our will with His. At the same time, God invites us to involve ourselves in His work by praying.

Sometimes all you have to do is ask the Lord once or twice for something that you really want. If the prayer request is in His perfect will for your life, He will answer your prayer simply after one or two prayer requests and that will be it. You will not have to get all worked up into any kind of major prevailing or travailing with Him.

> James 4:3
>
> Yet you do not have because you do not ask. You ask and do not receive, because you ask amiss, that you may spend it on your pleasures.

This verse gives us two major revelations. The first revelation is that you cannot receive something from God if you do not ask Him for it. We cannot expect God to come through for us if we do not petition Him in prayer.

The second revelation is that maybe your prayer request is not God's perfect will for your life. You may be asking for something that will not help you towards your divine destination.

All we have to do is be willing to stay humble and accountable in our walk with Him and never forget that we will need His help and guidance on a daily basis in order to fulfill our specific goals in life.

Be specific

> Philippians 4:6;19
>
> Be anxious for nothing, but in everything by prayer and supplication, with thanksgiving, let your requests be made known to God; And my God shall supply all your need according to His riches in glory by Christ Jesus.

Many people do not have their prayer answered because they do not know what they want. Over a period of time believers may change their prayer requests. God is not a God of confusion.

We need to be specific when we make our requests to God. We need to know where we are going with God and what we need for our spiritual journey. Specific prayer requests will ensure that God will supply everything we need in order to fulfill our divine purpose as long as it in accordance with God's plan for our lives. God always knows what is best for us.

Pray in the name of Jesus

> John 14:13-14
> And whatever you ask in My name, that I will do, that the Father may be glorified in the Son. If you ask anything in My name, I will do it.

The name of Jesus is of utmost importance in intercession. Without His name we are not able to do anything nor do we have the right to ask Him for anything in prayer.

During the time the Bible was written, a person's name described who that person was and what you could expect from that person.

To pray in the name of Jesus is to pray with all His power and authority. To pray in Jesus' Name is the key to all the power and promises of God.

Pray in faith

> Mark 11:22-24
>
> So Jesus answered and said to them, "Have faith in God. For assuredly, I say to you, whoever says to this mountain, 'Be removed and be cast into the sea,' and does not doubt in his heart, but believes that those things he says will be done, he will have whatever he says. Therefore I say to you, whatever things you ask when you pray, believe that you receive them, and you will have them."

It is important to understand that God does answer every prayer. There are different answers to each request. Sometimes the answer is yes. The answer could also be no. The prayer could also be answered later on or after a long period of time has elapsed.

Knowing this makes it is easier to pray in faith because you understand that God loves you and hears you.

To pray in faith is to know without a doubt that God cares about you and that He is listening to you. It is having the complete assurance that what you are asking for will come to pass.

You must believe that prayer is powerful and effective. While you may not see the direct outcome of your prayer, you know that your prayer will change something.

Be open and honest with God. Pray what you mean from your heart, because God knows your secrets anyway. Open and honest communication will free you and create a bond with Him.

Genuine, authentic faith must be definite and free of doubt. Faith is increased by exercise and is nourished by trials. Faith grows by reading and meditating upon the Word of God and thrives in an atmosphere of prayer.

Prayer is absolutely dependent upon faith. It has no existence apart from it and accomplishes nothing unless it is its inseparable companion. Faith makes prayer effectual and must precede it.

Before prayer requests are made known to God, faith must have gone on ahead and must have asserted its belief in the supernatural power of God.

Faith causes prayer to work and gives the assurance that there is a loving High Priest who awaits the prayers of His children.

Faith opens the way for prayer to approach God and accompanies prayer at every step of its journey. It is faith which turns the asking into obtaining. The spiritual life into which a believer is led by prayer is a life of faith. Faith makes prayer strong and gives it patience to wait on God.

We need to be constantly reminded that faith is the one inseparable condition of successful praying.

Pray according to God's will

> Isaiah 55:8-9
>
> "For my thoughts are not your thoughts, neither are your ways my ways," declares the Lord. "As the heavens are higher than the earth so are my ways higher than your ways and my thoughts than your thoughts."

We must align our will with the will of God. God knows what is best for us. Through prayer we learn to discern God's will and submit to it.

This happens especially when He does not grant us certain requests because some of the things we ask for are not His will for us.

If we do not understand this principle we will become depressed and confused and go about murmuring and eventually grow cold and indifferent towards Him.

The condition for effectual prayer is that there should be no conflict between God's will and ours. We must realize that the will of God alone is good and perfect.

To pray according to God's will requires you to surrender your own will to the will of God.

Prayer that is prayed according to the will of God always puts God and His desires and purposes first. It is an unselfish prayer.

Pray with expectation

> Jeremiah 33:3
> Call to Me and I will answer you and tell you great and mighty things you do not know.
>
> Psalm 5:3
> My voice You shall hear in the morning, O LORD; in the morning I will direct it to You. And I will look up.

Always pray with expectation or else there is no point in praying at all. There are many people who pray without having any expectation of receiving.

Expectation is the key to receiving all the good things God has for you. Faith is required to receive from God and our expectation is proof of our faith.

Not only must we pray according to God's will, but we must be in God's will if we expect Him to hear and answer us.

Be obedient

> 1 John 3:21-22
> Dear friends, if our hearts do not condemn us, we have confidence before God and receive from Him anything we ask, because we obey His commands and do what pleases Him.

Sometimes disobedience is considered a minor matter when it comes to prayer but effective prayer always accompanies obedience. Disobedience is sin and it hinders our prayers. Prayer and obedience go hand in hand. We must continue to obey God and keep our hearts free from sin.

Victory in prayer has more to do with obedience than praying. We must obey the prompting of the Holy Spirit instead of only praying and not obeying.

Prayer also generates the power to pray more, and hence the cycle continues by His grace. The only thing that can stop this cycle of effective praying is giving in to temptation and sin that the enemy brings through different circumstances.

Live a life of holiness

> 1 Peter 1:16
> Be holy, for I am holy.

Holiness is important to God and should be to us. That which is holy belongs to God. Whatever belongs to God is holy.

Holiness implies being set apart and includes living in a special way that is different from the rest of the world.

In order to live a life of holiness we need to be partakers of God's holiness. We live in an evil world, but our lives must be different from the lives of other people in the world.

We will continue to be holy as long as we live a life of holiness. That is the way of obedience and conformity with God's ways and spiritual laws. Living a life of compromise and sin will most certainly hinder our prayers.

Examples of effective praying

The Bible is filled with examples of prayers that were powerful and effective.

- Moses had numerous intercessory prayers that God answered, even when He had told Moses that He would follow a different course of action to what Moses requested of Him.
- A repentant Samson prayed for one more opportunity to fulfill his life's task of defeating the Philistines. God answered this prayer by giving him strength to pull down the pillars of the building in which they were celebrating the power of their gods.
- The prophet Elijah had at least four powerful prayers answered, all of which brought glory to the God of Israel.
- King Hezekiah became sick and was told by Isaiah that he would die. Feeling his life and work were incomplete, Hezekiah prayed intensely for God to give him more time. God sent Isaiah back to Hezekiah, assuring him of healing and fifteen more years of life.

- Daniel prayed to the Lord in the den of lions asking for deliverance from their mouths and the Lord granted his request.
- The early Christians prayed earnestly for Peter's release from prison and God sent an angel to free him.

Such examples should fill us with desire and faith to pray effectively according to the principles outlined in the Scriptures.

Just a thought....

Someone once said to me "All things are possible – unfortunately." 100% answered prayer. Could that ever be a possibility in a fallen world? I believe it. If we follow the principles set out in God's Word, each and every one of us have the potential to pray prayers that have a 100% success rate. But remember to pray by the rules!

CHAPTER 2

All Kinds of Prayer

> Ephesians 6:18
> Praying always with all prayer and supplication in the Spirit.

There are different kinds of prayer mentioned and modeled throughout the Bible. They are discussed in different places in the Bible and in different ways.

All prayer is communication with God, but as with communication with people, there are many ways and methods of communication. To really understand what the Bible says about prayer, one must keep in mind the kind of prayer that is being discussed in each passage of God's Word.

Prayer walking

> Joshua 1:3
> Every place that the sole of your foot will tread upon I have given you, as I said to Moses.

Prayer walking is the practice of praying on location and is a type of intercessory prayer that involves walking to or near a particular place while praying. It can be defined as praying on site with insight.

Prayer walking is prayer that is targeted for the place you are walking and is simply praying in the very places where you expect God to answer your prayers.

The concept of prayer walking brings the person who is praying into direct contact with the community for whom they are passionately praying.

Actually seeing your prayer target can also inspire you with the right way to pray so that your prayer will be the most effective.

Prayer walks are taken by individuals, groups, and even whole churches.

This is an exciting way of stimulating prayer within the congregation and is a way of taking prayer to the people. It can break down the wall between the church and the community.

Prayer walking is a relatively new phenomenon, the origin of which is not clear. There is no Biblical model for prayer walking. But since walking was the major mode of transportation in Bible times, clearly people must have walked and prayed at the same time.

Prayer walking helps sensitize you to the issues. The sounds, sights, and smells will help to engage your spirit in intercession.

It can include walking around your neighborhood or a city wide prayer walk. This is usually organized and participated in by several churches.

Corporate prayer

> Psalm 133:1-3
>
> Behold, how good and how pleasant it is for brethren to dwell together in unity! It is like the precious oil upon the head, Running down on the beard, The beard of Aaron, Running down on the edge of his garments. It is like the dew of Hermon, Descending upon the mountains of Zion; For there the LORD commanded the blessing- Life forevermore.

Corporate prayer is probably one of the most neglected and misunderstood forms of prayer we find described in the Bible. Usually, when Christians gather together to pray, a whole array of prayers are offered by each individual instead of the group simply bringing a few focused prayers in complete unison before the Lord.

Despite some of the misconceptions that exist, proper corporate prayer is extremely powerful when we truly appreciate its value and perform it correctly.

On the Day of Pentecost, God poured out His Spirit mightily on a group of believers who had being praying together for ten days. The Bible tells us that they were also in one accord, which means they were in agreement and passionate about the same thing.

Each individual musical instrument on its own may make a wonderful sound. However, when all the instruments are played together, they form one beautiful harmonious sound carrying with it much deeper emotion and meaning.

The same happens when we agree together in corporate prayer. When we all pray together at the same time for the same thing, the power of the Holy Spirit is released in a much greater way, bringing swift breakthroughs and answers to prayer.

As Christian believers we must seek the Lord corporately and apply the principles of corporate prayer diligently and accurately.

Corporate prayer for all people will bring the presence of God into manifestation on the earth and bring change and revival where religious and demonic strongholds have held cities, nations and continents captive for thousands of years.

Corporate prayer is an important part of the life of the church, along with worship, sound doctrine, communion, and fellowship. The early church met regularly to learn the doctrine of the apostles, to break bread, and to pray together.

This is why every single Bible-based, Spirit-filled, Christian church should have intercessory prayer teams who are mighty and powerful prayer warriors and who know how to powerfully and effectively pray to God the Father.

These kinds of mighty prayer warriors can pull down major miracles from heaven and every church should identify and utilize them.

The effects are very positive when we pray together with other believers. Corporate prayer edifies and unifies us as we share our common faith. The same Holy Spirit who dwells within each believer knits us together in a unique bond of fellowship found nowhere else in life.

Prayers of praise and worship

> Psalm 138:2
> I will worship toward Your holy temple, And praise Your name For Your lovingkindness and Your truth; For You have magnified Your word above all Your name.

Praise and worship go hand in hand.

David was a man that spent a lot of time in the presence of God ministering to God in prayer. Most of the Psalms he wrote expressed his love and devotion for God through praise and worship.

One of the beauties of Christianity is the personal relationship we have with God. To praise and worship God is to have intense love and admiration for Him and to express admiration and thanksgiving to Him.

THE FIVE-FOLD PRAYER

Praise and worship brings us into the presence of God. When we praise God in the midst of seemingly negative situations we are affirming our faith in Him. This pleases God and helps our faith.

Praising and worshiping God is not about a ritual or prayer repetition but requires a total commitment of our body, mind and spirit. It is about exalting, adoring and acknowledging the God of the Bible. To praise and to worship God is to express our love and awe of who He is.

To many, praise and worship is associated with singing. However, it should become part of our everyday lives and especially during times of prayer. In praise and worship, you will sometimes need to resort to prayer to do battle with the enemy. True praise and worship involves faith, hope, and love. These are powerful weapons in the Christian armory.

God alone is worthy of our devotion, praise and worship. He is God, our Creator, and we are commanded to praise and worship Him. A life of praise and worship fills our deepest needs and brings great joy to God.

The best way that we can praise and worship God is with our every thought and action. Many people think that praise and worship is only singing songs at church, but it is so much more. It is important to spend time praising and worshipping God when we separate ourselves in the presence of God.

Prayers of praise and worship are considered to be very effective because it is all about God. During this time of devotion, our praise and worship is directed to God. We ask for nothing and focus on nothing but God Himself.

Prayer walking offers many opportunities for praise and worship.

Prayers of binding and loosing

> Matthew 16:19
> And I will give you the keys of the kingdom of heaven, and whatever you bind on earth will be bound in heaven, and whatever you loose on earth will be loosed in heaven.

> Mark 3:27
> No one can enter a strong man's house and plunder his goods, unless he first binds the strong man. And then he will plunder his house.

Only true Christians have this power and authority to bind evil and loose God's purposes in the name of Jesus. Jesus explained that we must first bind the strongman before we can plunder his house.

Everything that is loosed or bound must be in accordance with God's Word.

When something is loosed on the earth, its activities and presence are permitted and declared lawful. It is important for

Christians to know what areas of their lives are in bondage and should identify any open door that allowed the enemy to move into that area of their life.

It is always a good idea to become familiar with the various ways the enemy can gain access into a person's life. Most times a person can identify what caused the bondage and when it started.

Christians are taught that they must take authority over demon spirits in the name of Jesus. They must renounce any activities that opened the door through which they have been able to enter and bind their activities. We have the power and authority to bind evil and loose God's plans in any situation.

Prayers of agreement

> Matthew 18:19-20
> Again I say to you that if two of you agree on earth concerning anything that they ask, it will be done for them by My Father in heaven. For where two or three are gathered together in My name, I am there in the midst of them.

The prayer of agreement is another real powerful one to add to your arsenal of prayer strategies that you can apply to your life.

Two people have to be in perfect agreement with one another on the specific prayer request that they want to put before the Lord. This means that two people are approaching the throne of God and they are praying for the exact same thing.

Jesus promises that He will personally be in the midst of two or three believers who come together in His name to pray about a particular matter.

God can release many powerful miracles when individual believers approach the Lord in their own personal prayer life with Him. It is not always necessary to call on other Christians every single time you have something to pray about.

However, there is also a definite time and place for united group prayer. There will be times that you will want to call on other believers to storm the gates of heaven with you.

Jesus Himself says that He will literally be in the midst of any two or three believers who are praying in unity and agreement with one another. That is a powerful prayer secret!

If God is going to want to team you up with other believers from time to time, you will need good Christian friends who you can approach and ask to pray with you in unity and agreement.

Prayers of intercession

> Isaiah 59:16
> He saw that there was no man, and wondered that there was no intercessor; therefore His own arm brought salvation for him.

Psalm 106:23
Moses His chosen one stood before Him in the breach, to turn away His wrath, lest He destroy them.

Acts 12:5
So Peter was kept in prison, but the church was earnestly praying to God for him.

Quite simply put, intercessory prayer is the act of praying on behalf of others. Praying for others is at the root of our Christian faith. Jesus Himself prayed for others. Prayers of intercession are to be offered on behalf of other people and by interceding we reach out to God on behalf of others.

The background for understanding prayers of intercession is found in the Old Testament example of the Levitical priesthood. The priest's responsibility was to stand between a righteous God and sinful man bringing them together at the place of the blood sacrifice.

Under the New Covenant, Jesus Christ is our model for intercessory prayer. Jesus stands before God between the Father and sinful man, just as the Old Testament priests did.

Jesus brings sinful man and a righteous God together at the place of the blood sacrifice for sin. No longer is the blood of animals necessary as it was in the Old Testament. We can now approach God on the basis of the blood of Jesus that was shed on the cross of Calvary for the remission of sins. Because of the blood of Jesus, we can approach God boldly and without timidity.

Jesus was an intercessor while He was here on earth. He prayed for those who were sick and possessed by demons. He prayed for His disciples. Jesus continued His ministry of intercession even after His death and resurrection when He returned to Heaven. He now serves as our intercessor in Heaven.

The Bible records many cases of people standing up for others before God.

- Abraham pleaded with God for the well-being of the people of Sodom. Instead of being overcome with his own needs, Abraham prayed for those around him. He took the initiative to step forward before God on behalf of his neighbors in Sodom. He cared enough to do it, even although he knew how thoroughly wicked Sodom was and how angry God was about it.
- Moses also stepped in when God was angry by standing in the gap and offering his own life for that of his nation.
- Isaiah prayed with King Hezekiah to save the nation from defeat and destruction at the hands of Assyria. The armies were suddenly turned back.
- Nehemiah prayed to God to bring about the rebuilding of Jerusalem and the restoration of his people.
- Stephen's last words were an intercession on behalf of those who were killing him.

- The church prayed fervently for Peter while he was imprisoned.
- It is Paul's regular intercession for the church and its people which sets the usual pattern for our own intercessory prayers.

As they took their concerns to God, the key motivation behind these giants of faith was compassion. They loved the people so much that they dared to take on God on their behalf.

The Bible is clear that all Christians are called to be intercessors. All Christians have the Holy Spirit in their hearts and, just as He intercedes for us in accordance with God's will, we are to intercede for one another. This is not a privilege limited to an exclusive Christian elite but a command to all.

God calls all Christians to be intercessors. It is God's desire that every believer be active in intercessory prayer.

Intercessors also pray for world, national, and local political leaders. This follows in the tradition of the early church's prayers for the Roman authorities.

Prayers of petition

> 1 Samuel 1:17
>
> The Eli answered and said "Go in peace and the God of Israel grant your petition that you have asked Him."

1 John 5:15
And we know that He hears us, whatever we ask, we know that we have the petitions that we have.

A petition is a formal written request addressed to a higher authority having the power to grant it. A petition prayer is a formal written request to God regarding a situation you need help with. The petition is written down on paper and presented to the Lord.

It is used for special prayer requests which you should always bring with you when you pray as a reminder to the Lord until that prayer is answered.

Prayers of petition are also referred to as prayers of supplication.

Believers are encouraged to write their prayer requests down. Every time you pray, present these requests to the Lord until they are answered. Write down the date when you made the request and record the date the Lord answered that prayer. It serves as a wonderful testimony and builds a history of the miracles you have experienced through answered prayer.

I was at the bedside of a wonderful woman of God after she passed away. Next to her bed was her prayer book that had many pages of prayer requests which she had written down over a number of years. I was really blessed to see that next to almost every prayer request she had written the words "answered" with the date.

When we implement prayers of petition, it keeps our faith alive knowing no matter what our need is, we have a prayer history with the Lord and the results are positive.

Making war with prophesies

> 1 Timothy 1:18
> This charge I commit to you, son Timothy, according to the prophecies previously made concerning you, that by them you may wage the good warfare.
>
> Habakkuk 2:2-3
> Then the Lord answered me and said: "Write the vision and make it plain on tablets, That he may run who reads it. For the vision is yet for an appointed time; But at the end it will speak, and it will not lie. Though it tarries, wait for it; Because it will surely come, It will not tarry.

Paul encouraged Timothy to wage warfare with the prophecies he received until they come to pass. It is important to write your prophecies down, because they define your spiritual future. They are very important and sometimes have a lot of detail which is impossible to remember.

The most powerful prayer anyone can pray is to pray in accordance with God's will. Prophecies which have been confirmed and which we are assured of, define God's will and purpose for our lives.

I have received many personal prophecies over the years. I have a prophetic journal and write all my prophecies down with the date I received them. I always bring my journal with me into my prayer room.

At times God has given me a prophetic dream. When I wake up I write down all the details, because dreams normally fade away very quickly. I have had many instances where pictures and images were involved. I have sketched these images so that they represent what I saw in my dream.

Taking your prophecies and praying them into manifestation is a powerful prayer that every Christian should pray. If you have never received a prophetic word from the Lord, do not go looking for one. The Lord knows when and where to bring every resource to you that is necessary for your divine purpose, especially when you have an intimate relationship with Him.

The Lord's prayer

>Matthew 6:9-13
>In this manner, therefore, pray:
>Our Father in heaven
>Hallowed be Your name
>Your kingdom come
>Your will be done on earth as it is in heaven
>Give us this day our daily bread.
>And forgive us our debts, as we forgive our debtors

> And do not lead us into temptation, But deliver us from the evil one. For Yours is the kingdom and the power and the glory forever
> Amen.

When the disciples asked Jesus to teach them to pray Jesus responded with what we know as the Lord's Prayer.

The fact that the disciples requested a model for praying shows us that we do not have to feel guilty when we do not understand prayer and need help with it. We seem to think we should have a built in instinct when it comes to knowing everything about prayer. The disciples were with Jesus every day and saw how He prayed. Yet even they needed help with prayer.

Though we memorize it as a set formula, the Lord's Prayer should not be repeated mechanically or without thought. Its purpose is to awaken and stimulate our faith.

We generally pray this prayer word for word, which is good, but it mainly teaches us what our own prayers should include when we go before God. Always remember that prayer is a personal relationship with God.

f. Our Father in heaven

Here we recognize that this prayer is to God. He is the Father of all and He resides in heaven. We are linked through God to one another as one family.

By telling us to call God "Father" Jesus moves us from images of a remote God to an image of a God who is with us constantly.

God sees us as if we were a daughter or a son. And we, on our part, can approach God in the familiar confident way a child approaches a loving parent. What is more, we approach God through Jesus Christ.

g. Hallowed be Your name

This is another word for holy. We are telling God that we know He is holy. He then becomes our standard of holiness.

h. Your Kingdom come

This is acknowledging that Jesus will come again to earth one day and His Kingdom will be marked by peace and justice. It will one day be established in visible form.

The centrality of the Kingdom message is clear in the New Testament.

i. Your will be done on earth as it is in heaven

This is stating that we know God is in control of all things in and under heaven.

The world will be transformed into a place where God reigns and where things are done in accordance with God's standards.

j. Give us today our daily bread

God provides for our physical needs. He provides food to sustain us, gives us shelter, and provides ways for us to take care of ourselves. We depend on God's grace to give us what we need.

Like the Hebrews gathering manna each day in the wilderness, we cannot store up what we need from God. Yesterday's experience with God cannot nourish us today.

k. Forgive us our debts as we have also forgiven our debtors

Not everyone is able to pay back a debt. It is in this way that we can never repay Jesus for the sacrifice He made for us, but He died for us anyway.

But He asks that we forgive other people when they cannot or will not pay us back for something we have lent to them, no matter what it may be.

Forgiveness often does not come easily. Many of us find it difficult to forgive others.

Jesus said that if we do not forgive others, we cannot experience God's forgiveness ourselves.

Nursing hurts from the past takes energy and forgiving frees us to use that energy to live fully and abundantly in the present.

l. And lead us not into temptation but deliver us from the evil one

Here we are asking God to keep our hearts pure and to help us stay away from the things that tempt us to do wrong.

Life is not easy. It is a daily battle. Trials like sickness and failure can crush our spirits. Temptations can entice us and even destroy us.

We ask God to keep us from failing when we are tested, to help us to know the right thing to do and to deliver us from the evil which awaits us in life.

The prayer of Jabez

Jabez prayed a four-part prayer that changed his entire life. Not much was said about Jabez but his prayer, which is recorded in only one verse in the Bible, has had a great impact on the entire Body of Christ.

THE FIVE-FOLD PRAYER

> 1 Chronicles 4:10
>
> And Jabez called on the God of Israel saying, "Oh that You would bless me indeed, and enlarge my territory, that Your hand would be with me, and that You would keep me from evil, that I may not cause pain!" So God granted him what he requested.

Here are his four requests:

- Bless Me
- Enlarge my territory
- That Your hand would be with me
- Keep me from evil, that I may not cause pain

Jabez's goal in his prayer was to live free from sorrow. We only have a brief account of who he was and what he did. The theme of this story is that Jabez was a man who believed in prayer. His prayer is recorded for us as an outstanding example of a man whose life was changed by the power of prayer.

All we know about the birth of Jabez is that he was from the tribe of Judah and that his mother named him Jabez because she had a very painful birth with him.

The Prayer of Jabez discusses the important place of prayer in the Christian life. All Christians should pray.

It also encourages Christians to focus on prayer for spiritual blessing, expanded outreach, guidance, and protection from evil. Jesus touched on all these things in His pattern of prayer.

At the end of the verse it is clear that God approved of this prayer by granting Jabez's petition.

Quiet time

> Mark 1:35
>
> Now in the morning, having risen a long while before daylight, He went out and departed to a solitary place; and there He prayed.

Quiet time is one of the most essential aspects of our Christian lives.

Without daily regular quiet time, our spiritual lives can be seriously malnourished just as our bodies can be malnourished without proper food and water.

The Bible teaches us how to spend quiet time with God. Jesus gave us examples in the Gospels where He stepped away from the limelight and retreated to a quiet place to commune with His Father. These quiet times spent with God had some very important elements in common.

Each time Jesus wanted to spend time with His Father, He always retreated to a secluded area free from distractions. He could talk with God and listen to Him as well. The same is true of us. Our quiet times with God should be in a place where we are alone with no distractions.

Quiet time with God is also a time to read God's Word.

THE FIVE-FOLD PRAYER

Jesus often quoted from God's Word in His quiet times. It is through daily prayer and reading God's Word that we will grow in our walk with God.

It is important to set time aside each day to talk with God because this is the best way to draw close to Him. It is a time we spend with God and no one else is with us.

A quiet time is a way of maintaining fellowship with God and evaluating our lifestyle. It is a way of building spiritual strength, becoming more sensitive to God's leadership, and applying His Word to our actions.

Jesus withdrew from the crowd and then withdrew from His disciples to spend time alone with His father. Jesus spent time with His Heavenly Father seeking fellowship, strength, and guidance. If God's Son needed to spend time with Him, how much more do you need to spend time with Him? Having a quiet time means you will become more like Christ as you follow His example and as you receive His power through prayer and the Word.

Moses spent many days alone with God on the mountain. His assistant Joshua walked up the mountain with him to a certain point. Moses then told him to wait as he carried on up the mountain to be alone with God.

Just a thought…..

There are so many kinds of prayer and so many aspects to prayer. God is good and has helped us by giving us so many different resources to know Him more. But remember, prayer is not a formula. If you pursue intimacy you will catch everything.

CHAPTER 3

The Prayer Life of Jesus

Jesus was a great example of prayer. Even though He was the Son of God, Jesus prayed while He was on earth. There was also an unmistaken quality about the prayer life of Jesus. The life of Jesus had many marked characteristics, but nothing is more marked than His prayerfulness.

Prayer should be important to us because it was important to Jesus. Jesus is our greatest model of intercessory prayer. Prayer accompanied every event in His life.

Jesus prayed in connection with the simplest events of everyday life. No matter how busy He was, He always took time to pray. He did not allow the crowds or the demands of ministry to take time from His prayer life.

Jesus believed that prayer works. He believed and acted on the confidence that God answered His prayers.

> Matthew 7:7-11
> Ask and it will be given to you; seek and you will find; knock and the door will be opened to you. For everyone who asks receives; he who seeks finds; and to him who knocks, the door will be opened. Which of you, if his son

asks for bread, will give him a stone? Or if he asks for a fish, will give him a snake? If you, then, though you are evil, know how to give good gifts to your children, how much more will your Father in heaven give good gifts to those who ask Him?

We can have that same confidence especially when we understand the mind and heart of Jesus and then pray accordingly. When our prayers are being answered it will only give us more confidence and boldness to pray for even greater things.

As we incorporate these practices of prayer that Jesus modeled into our Christian walk, we will begin to see the power of prayer become a living reality in our lives just as it was in the life of Jesus.

Jesus prayed the will of the Father

Matthew 26:42

Again, a second time, He went away and prayed, saying, "O My Father, if this cup cannot pass away from Me unless I drink it, Your will be done."

Jesus prayed in perfect submission to the Father's will. We find Him moving to the Garden of Gethsemane and pouring out His soul in prayer. Here we find the great obedience of Jesus in prayer. He knew that God the Father could remove the cup of suffering. He stated that fact in His prayer. But He also went further by praying for God's will to be done. Jesus did not want His will to be done.

He was obedient and submitted to His Father's will. This kind of prayer is the most difficult kind of prayer. Yet Jesus prayed this at His moment of greatest agony.

Nothing pleases God more than to see us pray for His will to be done. We pray the perfect prayer when we pray in accordance to God's will

Jesus prayed before making decisions

> Luke 6:12-13
>
> Now it came to pass in those days that He went out to the mountain to pray, and continued all night in prayer to God. And when it was day, He called His disciples to Himself; and from them He chose twelve whom He also named apostles.

It is very important to spend time in prayer before making life changing decisions. Wrong decisions can destroy the purposes God has for our lives especially when it involves ministry.

Jesus took His ministry mandate very seriously and asked God before He implemented any structures. He spent a long time in prayer before appointing anyone to assist Him in ministry.

After this time in prayer, He appointed the twelve as His disciples.

THE FIVE-FOLD PRAYER

Prayer postures of Jesus

a. **Kneeling**

At times, Jesus prayed while kneeling.

> Luke 22:41
>
> He withdrew about a stone's throw beyond them, knelt down and prayed.

b. **Lying down**

At other times, He prayed on His face before God.

> Matthew 26:39
>
> Going a little farther, he fell with his face to the ground and prayed, "My Father, if it is possible, may this cup be taken from me. Yet not as I will, but as you will."

c. **Looking towards heaven**

> Matthew 14:19
>
> Then He commanded the multitudes to sit down on the grass. And He took the five loaves and the two fish, and looking up to heaven, He blessed and broke and gave the loaves to the disciples; and the disciples gave to the multitudes.

THE PRAYER LIFE OF JESUS

d. Sitting

> Mathew 26:26
>
> And as they were eating, Jesus took bread, blessed and broke it, and gave it to the disciples and said, "Take, eat; this is My body."

Jesus prayed persistently

> Matthew 26:44
>
> So He left them, went away again, and prayed the third time, saying the same words.

Failure to receive what you asked for the first time you prayed is not necessarily weak faith or failure.

Even Jesus had to persist in prayer by asking for the same thing three times.

Jesus taught others to pray

> Luke 11:1
>
> Now it came to pass, as He was praying in a certain place, when He ceased, that one of His disciples said to Him, "Lord, teach us to pray, as John also taught his disciples."

Jesus taught that prayer works. Jesus was praying at a certain place when one of His disciples asked Him to teach them to pray.

Jesus prayed for the glory

> John 12:28
> Father, glorify Your name." Then a voice came from heaven, saying, "I have both glorified it and will glorify it again."

Here Jesus is praying that He may be glorified. The Bible teaches us that Jesus brought glory on earth to God by completing the work God gave Him to do. Jesus prayed that the glory which He had with God before the world began may be restored.

Our lives should be such that it should glorify God. Our works and deeds should glorify God. Therefore when we pray we should pray that we will bring glory to God in everything we do.

Jesus travailed in prayer

> Hebrews 5:7-8
> Who, in the days of His flesh, when He had offered up prayers and supplications, with vehement cries and tears to Him who was able to save Him from death, and was heard because of His godly fear, though He was a Son, yet He learned obedience by the things which He suffered.

This teaches us that prayer is not always filled with sweet language and fine expressions. Many times prayer turns out to be a battle and can be accompanied by cries and tears.

Jesus prayed prayers of thanksgiving

> Matthew 11:25
>
> At that time Jesus answered and said, "I thank You, Father, Lord of heaven and earth, that You have hidden these things from the wise and prudent and have revealed them to babes.

Jesus gave thanks when He prayed. He set a model that we should follow. To fail to give thanks reflects on the condition of our relationship with God.

We should always be thankful and express thanks to God for each of those blessings and more.

Thanksgiving is essential to prayer because all that we are and that we have comes from a generous God.

Jesus prayed even when tired

> Mark 6:31; 33-35; 46
>
> And He said to them, "Come aside by yourselves to a deserted place and rest a while." For there were many coming and going, and they did not even have time to eat. But the multitudes saw them departing, and many knew Him and ran there on foot from all the cities. They arrived before them and came together to Him.
>
> And Jesus, when He came out, saw a great multitude and was moved with compassion for them, because they were like sheep not having a shepherd. So He began to teach them many things. When the day was now far spent, His

disciples came to Him and said, "This is a deserted place, and already the hour is late. And when He had sent them away, He departed to the mountain to pray.

Jesus had spent the entire day ministering to the crowds and performing miracles so that they could eat. It was very late in the day and He must have been tired.

But instead of resting, He spent time in prayer.

Jesus prayed early in the morning

Mark 1:35

Now in the morning, having risen a long while before daylight, He went out and departed to a solitary place; and there He prayed.

Jesus rose very early in the morning to pray.

Jesus prayed throughout the night

Luke 6:12

Now it came to pass in those days that He went out to the mountain to pray.

We need to spend more time with God in prayer. Jesus spent a whole night on a mountainside in prayer.

Jesus prayed for Himself

> Matthew 26:39
> He went a little farther and fell on His face, and prayed, saying, "O My Father, if it is possible, let this cup pass from Me; nevertheless, not as I will, but as You will."

Jesus was about to face those who would accuse Him falsely and who would then crucify Him. He needed strength and assurance because going to the cross was His choice.

His agony was greater in prayer than when He faced His enemies. He was calm when He faced them. He had prayed for Himself and submitted Himself to the Father's will and received the strength He needed to complete the work.

Jesus prayed for others

Love prompts us to pray for others. Jesus prayed for other people. But He did not pray for everyone. He did not pray for those who ultimately will not be saved.

a. He prayed for children

> Mark 10:13;16
> Then they brought little children to Him, that He might touch them. And He took them up in His arms, laid His hands on them, and blessed them.

When people came to Jesus with their little children, He prayed for them and blessed them.

b. He prayed for individuals

> Luke 22:31-32
> And the Lord said, "Simon, Simon! Indeed, Satan has asked for you, that he may sift you as wheat. But I have prayed for you, that your faith should not fail; and when you have returned to Me, strengthen your brethren."

Towards the end of His life Jesus informed Peter that Satan had asked to sift him as wheat. But Jesus added that He had prayed for Peter that his faith might not fail.

c. He prayed for His disciples

> John 17:9
> I pray for them. I do not pray for the world but for those whom You have given Me, for they are Yours.

Jesus prayed specially for all His disciples.

d. He prayed for believers throughout eternity

> John 17:20-21
> I do not pray for these alone, but also for those who will believe in Me through their word; that they all may be one, as You, Father, are in Me, and I in You; that they

also may be one in Us, that the world may believe that You sent Me.

Jesus prayed that every believer that would come to know Him in the future.

He also prayed for the unity of all believers. Only today do we realize the power and challenge of that prayer.

Jesus prayed with others

> Luke 9:28
> About eight days after Jesus said this, he took Peter, John and James with him and went up onto a mountain to pray.

Jesus balanced private and corporate prayer.

He not only prayed alone, but He also prayed with other people in communities and gatherings.

Praying with the people of God is foundational to worship. Praying with others helps identify our weaknesses and needs. It also strengthens private prayer.

Jesus prayed alone

> Luke 22:41
> And He was withdrawn from them about a stone's throw, and He knelt down and prayed.

> Mark 1:35
> Now in the morning, having risen a long while before daylight, He went out and departed to a solitary place; and there He prayed.

Jesus often withdrew from His disciples and the crowds to be alone to pray. He often went up on a mountainside or went to solitary or lonely places to pray.

This habit of Jesus teaches us that though we may pray while in a group or in a prayer meeting, there is a great need to withdraw and pray alone.

In order to do this, we need to find a place where we can pray in private without being hindered in any way.

Although corporate prayer is helpful for fellowship, there are times when we need to be alone. That is why Jesus rose up early and also went to solitary places to pray.

When life is unusually busy, we should find the time to withdraw to a solitary place to pray.

Jesus prayed before eating

> Luke 24:30
> Now it came to pass, as He sat at the table with them, that He took bread, blessed and broke it, and gave it to them.

Praying before meals reminds us that we are the beneficiaries of good things and that God has blessed us with food.

Jesus prayed openly over the loaves and fish.

Jesus prayed for His enemies

> Luke 23:34
>
> Jesus said, "Father, forgive them, for they do not know what they are doing."

Jesus prayed before His ministry started

> Luke 3:21-22
>
> When all the people were baptized, it came to pass that Jesus also was baptized; and while He prayed, the heaven was opened. And the Holy Spirit descended in bodily form like a dove upon Him, and a voice came from heaven which said, "You are My beloved Son; in You I am well pleased."

Jesus began His ministry by prayer. As John baptized Him in water, He prayed and was baptized with the Holy Spirit and was anointed by God for ministry.

Jesus thought it important to begin His public ministry with prayer. We too have significant beginnings in life and these should be marked by prayer. We need to follow His example and seek God's guidance and strength in prayer.

> Acts 10:38
>
> How God anointed Jesus of Nazareth with the Holy Spirit and with power, who went about doing good and healing all who were oppressed by the devil, for God was with Him.

If Jesus needed the anointing of the Holy Spirit before He ministered to people to meet their needs, how much more do we need the anointing? The surest way to receive this blessing is to pray and ask God for it.

Jesus prayed before ministering

> John 11:41
>
> Then they took away the stone from the place where the dead man was lying. And Jesus lifted up His eyes and said, "Father, I thank You that You have heard Me.

Before Jesus raised Lazarus from the dead, He prayed and thanked God for the miracle.

This same confidence is seen when Jesus gave thanks by looking up to heaven before He fed the five thousand and four thousand people respectively. We have to learn to have such confidence in our prayers.

THE PRAYER LIFE OF JESUS

Jesus prayed after He ministered

> Luke 10:17;21
>
> Then the seventy returned with joy, saying, "Lord, even the demons are subject to us in Your name." In that hour Jesus rejoiced in the Spirit and said, "I thank You, Father, Lord of heaven and earth, that You have hidden these things from the wise and prudent and revealed them to babes. Even so, Father, for so it seemed good in Your sight.

Jesus prayed after the great achievements and important crises in His life.

He prayed that He might recover His strength.

Jesus prayed before He died

> Luke 23:34;46
>
> Jesus said, "Father, forgive them, for they do not know what they are doing." And when Jesus had cried out with a loud voice, He said, "Father, 'INTO YOUR HANDS I COMMIT MY SPIRIT.' " Having said this, He breathed His last.

Jesus prayed in the last moments of His life. His last utterance before His death was a prayer. His life had been a life of prayer and came to a close with prayer.

Jesus prayed after He died

> Luke 24:30-31
>
> Now it came to pass, as He sat at the table with them, that He took bread, blessed and broke it, and gave it to them. Then their eyes were opened and they knew Him; and He vanished from their sight.

It is extraordinary to learn that even after Jesus died and rose again, He continued to pray.

Before He ascended to heaven, He prayed again for His disciples.

Jesus still prays for us today

> Hebrews 7:25
>
> Therefore He is also able to save to the uttermost those who come to God through Him, since He always lives to make intercession for them.

> Romans 8:26-27
>
> In the same way, the Spirit helps us in our weakness. We do not know what we ought to pray for, but the Spirit himself intercedes for us with groans that words cannot express. And he who searches our hearts knows the mind of the Spirit, because the Spirit intercedes for the saints in accordance with God's will.

THE PRAYER LIFE OF JESUS

Jesus never stops praying for us. He prays for us continually. He stands in the gap making petitions to God on our behalf. He is our representative and our mediator in heaven.

He is always at our disposal before the throne of heaven pleading our case and sharing our cause with the Father.

Just a thought.....

How amazing to learn that Jesus continued His prayer life even after His resurrection and after He received His glorious body. Prayer should be started and must never stop. It seems that prayer begins on earth and continues into eternity. There is always a good reason to start prayer, but no good reason to stop praying whether in this life or the life to come.

CHAPTER 4

Fasting

> Matthew 6:16-18
>
> Moreover, when you fast, do not be like the hypocrites, with a sad countenance. For they disfigure their faces that they may appear to men to be fasting. Assuredly, I say to you, they have their reward. But you, when you fast, anoint your head and wash your face, so that you do not appear to men to be fasting, but to your Father who is in the secret place; and your Father who sees in secret will reward you openly.

Fasting has been described as sacrificial prayer and is one of the most powerful weapons of spiritual warfare that God has given to His children.

Biblically fasting is not a dieting process but a decision to abstain from food in order to achieve spiritual strength, answers and direction.

Fasting is abstinence from food for a limited period of time and is observed for spiritual purposes. By fasting, the believer chooses to do without food for a set time. Food is one of the great blessings of God in our lives and fasting is a way of crucifying the flesh.

Biblical fasting, unlike fasting for medical or health reasons, must be done with an attitude of seriousness, humility and sincerity. It is not necessary for others to know we are fasting, because it is directed towards God.

When we fast, we willingly deprive our bodies of nourishment and the pleasurable taste of food. The body requires food for sustenance and therefore our hearts and minds must be totally focused and directed towards God so that He may be the full source of our strength during the period of fasting.

Fasting is voluntary and helps you to dedicate yourself completely to prayer. All who practice fasting testify to the value thereof.

The main purpose of fasting is to have fellowship with God. It is not to try to force God to do something against His will, but to conform yourself to God's will.

Fasting contributes to spiritual and mental alertness. When we fast, our minds and perception are sharper because we are focusing less on temporal things and more on eternal realities.

Through fasting we are telling God that we are serious in our prayer and signals earnestness and urgency. Many report an elevated spiritual clarity while on or shortly after an extended fast.

Christians should fast

We find many examples of fasting throughout the Bible.

In the Old Testament we find people fasting on various occasions. People would fast, pray and seek God when there were wars or serious disasters like long term droughts or plagues.

During the time of Jesus the Jews fasted often. Some Pharisees fasted twice a week. They would put on ashes, wear rough clothing, and walk barefoot. They would go to the marketplace so that everyone could see how pious and righteous they were. They were fasting to be seen and praised by people.

John the Baptist and his disciples also fasted. Prayer and fasting was practiced regularly by the early apostles as recorded in the book of Acts.

> Matthew 9:14-15
> Then the disciples of John came to Him, saying, "Why do we and the Pharisees fast often, but Your disciples do not fast?" And Jesus said to them, "Can the friends of the bridegroom mourn as long as the bridegroom is with them? But the days will come when the bridegroom will be taken away from them, and then they will fast.

Jesus prophesied that His disciples would fast and indicated that fasting would become a necessity when He was taken away. Jesus was speaking about the period between His ascension and His second coming, which covers the church period and which applies to all believers today.

The followers of Jesus enjoyed a close fellowship and friendship with Him. While He was with them, it was a time of joy. This was not a time of mourning, fasting or weeping but a time of celebration. Expressing grief by fasting would have been inappropriate at that time. Since Jesus was with them they had no need to draw closer to Him through fasting.

Fasting throughout history

There are a few individuals whose fasts are recorded in the Bible:

- Moses fasted for 40 days
- Jesus fasted for 40 days
- Elijah fasted for 40 days
- Daniel fasted for 21 days
- David fasted for 7 days
- Esther fasted for 3 days
- Paul fasted for 3 days

Others who fasted throughout church history:

- Martin Luther was criticized because he fasted too much
- John Calvin fasted and prayed until most of Geneva turned to God

- John Knox fasted and prayed. The wicked Queen Mary said she feared no weapon like she feared John Knox's prayers
- Jonathan Edwards who was God's instrument in the revival in New England, fasted and prayed
- John Wesley fasted twice a week
- Charles Finney was one of the greatest spiritual leaders in history and was a man who fasted and prayed
- D L Moody's ministry was marked by prayer and fasting

The purpose of fasting

When we study Scripture, we find many reasons why people fasted.

Repentance

> 1 Samuel 7:3;6
>
> Then Samuel spoke to all the house of Israel, saying, "If you return to the LORD with all your hearts, then put away the foreign gods and the Ashtoreths from among you, and prepare your hearts for the LORD, and serve Him only; and He will deliver you from the hand of the Philistines." So they gathered together at Mizpah, drew water, and poured it out before the LORD. And they fasted that day, and said there, "We have sinned against the LORD." And Samuel judged the children of Israel at Mizpah.

THE FIVE-FOLD PRAYER

The Bible records various instances where God's people repented of their evil deeds by fasting.

Israel experienced a time when they were defeated by the Philistines. They had captured the Ark of the Covenant from Israel which greatly humiliated them.

Samuel told the people to repent. They obeyed and fasted for one day. They cried out to God and God allowed them to defeat the Philistines.

Serious tragedy

> Judges 20:26
>
> Then all the children of Israel, that is, all the people, went up and came to the house of God and wept. They sat there before the LORD and fasted that day until evening; and they offered burnt offerings and peace offerings before the LORD.

In this example, the people fasted because of a serious tragedy. The tribe of Benjamin was engaged in a civil war against all the other tribes of Israel. Forty thousand people were killed, and in the midst of this great tragedy, the people fasted and prayed.

For salvation from the enemy

> 2 Chronicles 20:1-3
>
> It happened after this that the people of Moab with the people of Ammon, and others with them besides the

Ammonites, came to battle against Jehoshaphat. Then some came and told Jehoshaphat, saying, "A great multitude is coming against you from beyond the sea, from Syria; and they are in Hazazon Tamar" (which is En Gedi). And Jehoshaphat feared, and set himself to seek the LORD, and proclaimed a fast throughout all Judah.

Jehoshaphat called for a fast when a large army came to fight against him. As he and his people fasted and prayed, God provided supernatural deliverance.

To mourn

Daniel 10:2-3

In those days I Daniel was mourning three full weeks. I ate no pleasant bread, neither came flesh nor wine in my mouth, neither did I anoint myself at all, till three whole weeks were fulfilled.

God showed Daniel a vision of the future. When he saw this vision he started to mourn for three full weeks. He understood the matter but wanted a greater understanding of what he had seen. He embarked on a partial fast for a period of twenty one days. This is known as the Daniel fast and allowed his mind to be sharp and perceptive to the Holy Spirit.

Esther 4:1-3

When Mordecai learned all that had happened, he tore his clothes and put on sackcloth and ashes, and went out into the midst of the city. He cried out with a loud and bitter cry. He went as far as the front of the king's gate, for no one might enter the king's gate clothed with sackcloth. And in every province where the king's command and decree arrived, there was great mourning among the Jews, with fasting, weeping, and wailing; and many lay in sackcloth and ashes.

During the time of Queen Esther in the Bible, the king passed a law stating that anyone in the kingdom could kill every living Jew they encountered and then confiscate their property. The king was not aware that Queen Esther was a Jew.

Throughout the kingdom, the Jews began to fast with weeping and mourning. God supernaturally delivered the Jews and gave them favor throughout the kingdom because of Queen Esther.

For supernatural revelation

Exodus 34:28
And he was there with the Lord forty days and forty nights; he did not eat bread, nor drink water. And he wrote upon the tables the words of the covenant, the ten commandments.

Moses spent 40 days and nights fasting as the Lord gave him supernatural revelation all of which is contained in the first five books of the Bible and covers the story of creation.

Before ordaining ministers

> Acts 14:23
>
> So when they had appointed elders in every church, and prayed with fasting, they commended them to the Lord in whom they had believed.

Here we can see how important it is to first fast and pray before appointing anyone into leadership positions in ministry.

For humility

Fasting is a means of humbling ourselves before God.

> Ezra 8:21
>
> Then I proclaimed a fast there at the river of Ahava, that we might humble ourselves before our God, to seek from Him the right way for us and our little ones and all our possessions.

The book of Ezra tells how the king of Persia allowed the Jews to return to Jerusalem after their time in exile. In order to reconcile Israel back to God, Ezra proclaims a fast so that the nation can be reconciled to God once again.

> 1Kings 21:27-29
>
> So it was, when Ahab heard those words, that he tore his clothes and put sackcloth on his body, and fasted and lay in sackcloth, and went about mourning. And the word of the LORD came to Elijah the Tishbite, saying, "See how Ahab has humbled himself before Me? Because he has

humbled himself before Me, I will not bring the calamity in his days. In the days of his son I will bring the calamity on his house."

Even wicked people who are destined for destruction receive mercy from the Lord when they humble themselves and fast.

To avert judgment from the Lord

Jonah 3:6-10

Then word came to the king of Nineveh; and he arose from his throne and laid aside his robe, covered himself with sackcloth and sat in ashes. And he caused it to be proclaimed and published throughout Nineveh by the decree of the king and his nobles, saying, Let neither man nor beast, herd nor flock, taste anything; do not let them eat, or drink water. But let man and beast be covered with sackcloth, and cry mightily to God; yes, let every one turn from his evil way and from the violence that is in his hands. Who can tell if God will turn and relent, and turn away from His fierce anger, so that we may not perish? Then God saw their works, that they turned from their evil way; and God relented from the disaster that He had said He would bring upon them, and He did not do it.

God was about to destroy Nineveh. But Jonah called a fast to avert God's judgment upon the city.

The entire city of Nineveh, including animals, fasted upon hearing the pronouncement of judgment from the prophet Jonah and God spared them.

To resist the devil's temptations

> Luke 4:1-3
>
> Then Jesus, being filled with the Holy Spirit, returned from the Jordan and was led by the Spirit into the wilderness, being tempted for forty days by the devil. And in those days He ate nothing, and afterward, when they had ended, He was hungry. And the devil said to Him, "If You are the Son of God, command this stone to become bread."

Jesus fasted for forty days in the desert. He received divine preparation for His earthly ministry while fasting and enduring temptation.

For spiritual power to cast out demons

> Matthew 17:18-21
>
> And Jesus rebuked the demon, and it came out of him; and the child was cured from that very hour. Then the disciples came to Jesus privately and said, "Why could we not cast it out?" So Jesus said to them, "Because of your unbelief; for assuredly, I say to you, if you have faith as a mustard seed, you will say to this mountain, 'Move from here to there,' and it will move; and nothing will be impossible for you.

The disciples were praying for a child that was possessed by a demon but it would not come out. Prior to this, Jesus had already given His disciples the authority to heal the sick and to cast out demons in His Name, which they did successfully.

However, they were confronted with a demon that they could not cast out no matter how they tried. But Jesus spoke to the demon and it left.

Jesus knew the value of fasting, and it seems that He developed a lifestyle of prayer and fasting. It is clear that He had been fasting prior to this incident with the demon possessed boy.

To fulfill prophecy

> Luke 2:36-38
>
> Now there was one, Anna, a prophetess, the daughter of Phanuel, of the tribe of Asher. She was of a great age, and had lived with a husband seven years from her virginity; and this woman was a widow of about eighty-four years, who did not depart from the temple, but served God with fastings and prayers night and day. And coming in that instant she gave thanks to the Lord, and spoke of Him to all those who looked for redemption in Jerusalem.

God raised up Anna to fast and pray for eighty four years for the coming of Jesus in the flesh.

For the nation

> Daniel 9:2-3
>
> In the first year of his reign I, Daniel, understood by the books the number of the years specified by the word of the LORD through Jeremiah the prophet, that He would accomplish seventy years in the desolations of Jerusalem.

> Then I set my face toward the Lord God to make request by prayer and supplications, with fasting, sackcloth, and ashes.

When Daniel the prophet learned that Israel would be set free from slavery in Babylon after seventy years, he set himself to fast and pray for the release of Israel. He knew that the seventy years was almost up and as a result of Daniel fasting and praying, God freed Israel from captivity.

Even though Jeremiah had prophesied Israel's freedom, Daniel knew that God wanted someone to fast and pray for it. God respects our sovereignty and free will and will not do something on His own without someone asking Him. Daniel fasted and prayed and interceded for the people of Israel.

Receiving tragic news

> 1 Samuel 31:11-13
>
> Now when the inhabitants of Jabesh Gilead heard what the Philistines had done to Saul, all the valiant men arose and traveled all night, and took the body of Saul and the bodies of his sons from the wall of Beth Shan; and they came to Jabesh and burned them there. Then they took their bones and buried them under the tamarisk tree at Jabesh, and fasted seven days.

The people fasted on hearing of the tragic death of Saul and his children.

> Nehemiah 1:3-4
>
> And they said to me, "The survivors who are left from the captivity in the province are there in great distress and reproach. The wall of Jerusalem is also broken down, and its gates are burned with fire." So it was, when I heard these words, that I sat down and wept, and mourned for many days; I was fasting and praying before the God of heaven.

Nehemiah fasted when he heard of the deplorable condition of the city of Jerusalem and the disgraceful circumstances of the people of God living there.

National tragedies

> Joel 1:4;14
>
> What the chewing locust left, the swarming locust has eaten; What the swarming locust left, the crawling locust has eaten; And what the crawling locust left, the consuming locust has eaten. Consecrate a fast, Call a sacred assembly; Gather the elders And all the inhabitants of the land Into the house of the LORD your God, And cry out to the LORD.

A locust plague devastated the economy of Israel. The prophet Joel called upon his people to fast and pray.

Just a thought.....

There is a difference between Christians who pray and Christians who do not pray. There is also a difference between Christians who pray and Christians who fast and pray.

CHAPTER 5

A New Prayer Language

Restoration of a universal language

God created man in His own image. God's desire is to have an intimate fellowship with mankind so that they can have fellowship with Him and to coexist with each other with one universal language.

Throughout Biblical history, it is clear that God has always implemented an alternative plan whenever man transgresses God's original plan.

It started in the Garden of Eden when Adam and Eve sinned against God and which resulted in God driving them out from the place where the law of life abounded.

But the Lord immediately set in motion His alternative plan and made a way for Jesus to shed His blood for everyone so that the law of life could once again take effect over the law of sin and death.

> Genesis 3:15
>
> And I will put enmity between you and the woman and between your seed and her Seed, He shall bruise your head, and you shall bruise His heel.

Now let us look at a similar situation a number of years later.

> Genesis 11:1-5
>
> And the whole earth was of one language, and of one speech. And they said one to another; Let us make brick, and burn them thoroughly. And they had brick for stone, and slime had they for mortar. And they said, Let us build us a city and a tower, whose top may reach unto heaven; and let us make us a name, lest we be scattered abroad upon the face of the whole earth. And the Lord came down to see the city and the tower, which the children of men are building.

The people came together and were successful because they had a common purpose and a common language.

> Genesis 11:6
>
> And the LORD said, Behold, the <u>people are one</u>, and they have <u>all one language</u>; and this they begin to do: and now <u>nothing will be restrained from them, which they have imagined to do.</u>

This is an astounding statement made by God, acknowledging that with unity of purpose and language, mankind can achieve anything. In order to stop their evil plan, God destroyed their unity by confusing their language.

A NEW PRAYER LANGUAGE

> Genesis 11:7-9
>
> Go to, let us go down, and there confound their language, that they may not understand one another's speech. So the LORD scattered them abroad from thence upon the face of all the earth: and they left off to build the city.
>
> Therefore is the name of it called Babel; because the LORD did there confound the language of all the earth: and from thence did the LORD scatter them abroad upon the face of all the earth.

Sadly, God was excluded from their plans and hence from their lives. God did not feature prominently in their thoughts and their motives.

But just as God had an alternative plan following the failure in the Garden of Eden, God had an alternative plan following the failure at Babel. God's plan was to restore a universal language through His Holy Spirit.

> Acts 2:1-4
>
> When the Day of Pentecost had fully come, they were all with one accord in one place. And suddenly there came a sound from heaven, as of a rushing mighty wind, and it filled the whole house where they were sitting. Then there appeared to them divided tongues, as of fire, and one sat upon each of them. And they were all filled with the Holy Spirit and began to speak with other tongues, as the Spirit gave them utterance.

Let us look at certain similarities here in comparison to the efforts at Babel:

- They were all in one place
- They were all in one accord
- There was a common language (in the latter case, tongues)

When these three elements were present at Babel, this is what God declared:

"Now nothing they determine to do will be withheld from them.."

The only difference between Babel and Pentecost was that God was now the center of their purpose.

One only needs to read the book of Acts to see how this tongue talking breed of believers turned the world upside down for Jesus. Two thousand years later, Spirit-filled believers are turning nations around with the message of Jesus.

Speaking in tongues was common in the early New Testament church and was widespread. The same should apply to the present day Church if it is to succeed in its mission.

The outpouring of the Holy Spirit at Pentecost

> Acts 2:1-4
> When the Day of Pentecost had fully come, they were all with one accord in one place. And suddenly there came a sound from heaven, as of a rushing mighty wind, and it

filled the whole house where they were sitting. Then there appeared to them divided tongues, as of fire, and one sat upon each of them. And they were all filled with the Holy Spirit and began to speak with other tongues, as the Spirit gave them utterance.

The Bible tells us that there were 120 believers who spoke in tongues on the Day of Pentecost.

Since they were all speaking in foreign languages, they could not understand each other. Therefore, they were not talking to one another. They all began rejoicing and praising God in tongues at the same time. This noise drew a crowd. The people in the crowd recognized their native languages being spoken.

This crowd did not gather until they heard the noise of the 120 people all talking at the same time and rejoicing and praising God.

Many Christians assume that when the disciples spoke in tongues at Pentecost it was for the purpose of witnessing to this crowd in their native languages, but in reality the disciples were not talking to the crowd at all. The disciples were all together in a house, rejoicing and praising God in different languages. They were talking to God and were not sharing the Gospel in tongues. They were giving God praise in the Holy Spirit and were praying with the Spirit.

People sometimes use the account of Pentecost to prove that the main purpose of tongues in the first century was for the purpose of witnessing to foreigners in their native languages.

The purpose of tongues at Pentecost was not for sharing the Gospel with foreigners in their native languages. The Bible does not teach that speaking in tongues is for witnessing to foreigners. Those who spoke in tongues throughout the Book of Acts were praying directly to God in the Holy Spirit. In other words, the communication was going from earth up to heaven.

Every passage on tongues in the entire New Testament describes one or both of the following:

- A person delivers a public message in tongues to a group of people such as a church congregation which is then interpreted through the Holy Spirit either by the speaker or by someone in the congregation. This is known as the gift of tongues used in combination with the gift of interpretation. It is also referred to as the public use of tongues.
- A person prays in the Holy Spirit to God. When a person prays in the Spirit, this does not need to be interpreted into the local language because God always understands what the Holy Spirit is saying. Sometimes God gives us the interpretation of what we said in order to edify us or instruct us. This is known as praying with the Spirit.

The baptism in the Holy Spirit

> Romans 8:9
>
> But you are not in the flesh but in the Spirit, if indeed the Spirit of God dwells in you. Now if anyone does not have the Spirit of Christ, he is not His.

Every born again person already has the Holy Spirit. They are born of the Spirit and already have the Holy Spirit through regeneration.

However, the dimension of power that God wants for His children can only be reached through the baptism in the Holy Spirit. It is God's will that every Christian be baptized in the Holy Spirit and that they speak in tongues. Baptism in the Holy Spirit is not the same as regeneration.

Although the Bible does give examples of people who were baptized in the Spirit at the same time as their regeneration, this is not always what happens. The Book of Acts reveals that repentance, baptism in water and the baptism in the Holy Spirit do not necessarily happen in the same order all the time.

The Holy Spirit enters our human spirit when we are born again of the Spirit of God and Jesus comes into us by His Spirit. However, there is an empowering by the Holy Spirit which is distinct from being born of God.

THE FIVE-FOLD PRAYER

> John 20:22
> And when He had said this, He breathed on them, and said to them, "Receive the Holy Spirit".

The apostles received the Holy Spirit in regeneration before the ascension when Jesus breathed on them and they were born again of the Spirit through the resurrection of Jesus from the dead.

But this was before the day of Pentecost. Before Jesus ascended to heaven, He told them not to leave Jerusalem, but to wait there for the baptism in the Holy Spirit which would empower them for ministry.

They obeyed Jesus and ten days later, they were filled with the Holy Spirit on the Day of Pentecost.

In the case of the Apostles, the baptism in the Spirit and being born of the Spirit were two separate events. They were born of the Spirit when Jesus breathed on them before the ascension, but were baptized in the Spirit on the day of Pentecost after the ascension.

In the case of Paul, he met Jesus on the road to Damascus and confessed Him as Lord.

> Acts 9:17
> And Ananias went his way and entered the house; and laying his hands on him he said, "Brother Saul, the Lord Jesus, who appeared to you on the road as you came, has

sent me that you may receive your sight and be filled with the Holy Spirit."

Three days later, God instructed Ananias to lay hands on Saul so that he would receive his sight and that he could be filled with the Holy Spirit.

The Baptism in the Holy Spirit gives us the same possibilities of relationship to the Father and power in ministry as Jesus had on earth. God wants us to move into these possibilities.

> Acts 1:8
> But you shall receive power when the Holy Spirit has come upon you; and you shall be witnesses to Me in Jerusalem, and in all Judea and Samaria, and to the end of the earth.

The main purpose of the baptism in the Holy Spirit is to multiply Jesus' earthly ministry of preaching, healing and casting out demons so that He can touch the whole world with His love and His power.

Praying with the Spirit

Praying with the Spirit or praying in tongues connects our spirit with the Spirit of God. Praying in tongues ensures that God's will is perfected in a believer's life.

Since the Bible commands us to pray with the Spirit, it is important for us to learn what this means so that we can be obedient to God.

Whenever the Bible speaks about praying with the Spirit or singing with the Spirit, it always involves tongues. Some scholars believe that groaning in the Spirit also involves tongues. Praying in tongues is a Holy Spirit inspired speech in a language unknown to the speaker.

> 1 Corinthians 13:1
> Though I speak with the tongues of men and of angels....

It can be tongues which are heavenly and which are not spoken by any person on earth or it can be an earthly language like Portuguese, but which is not known to the speaker.

We see an example of this in the New Testament when the Holy Spirit was poured out at Pentecost on the 120. They were speaking earthly languages, because the people who heard them understood the language.

> Acts 2:7-11
> Then they were all amazed and marveled, saying to one another, "Look, are not all these who speak Galileans? And how is it that we hear, each in our own language in which we were born? Parthians and Medes and Elamites, those dwelling in Mesopotamia, Judea and Cappadocia, Pontus and Asia, Phrygia and Pamphylia, Egypt and the parts of Libya adjoining Cyrene, visitors from Rome, both Jews and proselytes, Cretans and Arabs-we hear them

speaking in our own tongues the wonderful works of God."

Many people think that speaking in tongues is foolish. But this is not the case. You could be speaking in a language that somebody can understand. This however occurs on very rare occasions. Generally, when a person speaks in tongues, they are speaking in a heavenly language and if the tongue is spoken in a corporate setting, it should be interpreted for the edification and exhortation of the gathering.

Many people wonder whether the devil can understand tongues. Well if a person is speaking in somebody else's language, then the devil certainly can understand the tongue. He understands every language which is spoken on earth so it can be assumed that he also understands when a heavenly language is spoken. He may understand the meaning of the words, but that does not mean he understands the message.

That is why when you pray in the Holy Spirit the devil may understand the words but he does not understand the meaning or the mysteries that are being spoken. Only God can understand the entire context of the tongues that are being spoken because the Bible teaches that when a believer speaks in a tongue, he or she speaks to God and to no one else.

> 1 Corinthians 14:2
> But he who speaks in a tongue does not speak to men but to God, for no-one understands him; however, in the spirit he speaks mysteries.

This means that although the devil may understand the tongue, he does not understand what is being said. For example, if two people are having a conversation in English and an outsider who is English listens to the conversation, that person may not know the context of what is being discussed.

The foolish things of God

> 1 Corinthians 1:20-24;27
> Where is the wise? Where is the scribe? Where is the disputer of this age? Has not God made foolish the wisdom of this world? For since, in the wisdom of God, the world through wisdom did not know God, it pleased God through the foolishness of the message preached to save those who believe. For Jews request a sign, and Greeks seek after wisdom; but we preach Christ crucified, to the Jews a stumbling block and to the Greeks foolishness, but to those who are called, both Jews and Greeks, Christ the power of God and the wisdom of God. But God has chosen the foolish things of the world to put to shame the wise, and God has chosen the weak things of the world to put to shame the things which are mighty.

The things of God's Spirit cannot be processed by the human mind because it is beyond human understanding.

Speaking in tongues may sound foolish but it invokes the power of God.

There are four foolish things of God which releases the supernatural power of God.

a. The gospel message

Paul tells us that preaching the message of Jesus Christ is a foolish gospel, but it is the power of God to save sinners from eternal death.

b. The tithe

It is sometimes difficult for Christians to understand that when it comes to tithing, 90 is greater than 100. When applied, it releases the power of God's provision

c. The local church

Many Christians do not join a local church because they think the institution is foolish and unnecessary. However, nothing of spiritual value will be added to your life outside the local church. Submitting to the leadership of a church activates the power of God for our individual destinies and purposes.

d. Tongues

Speaking in tongues sounds so foolish and it is for that reason many Christians do not speak or pray in tongues. However, it activates a power that unfolds the secrets and mysteries that God has in His heart for each and every one of His children.

Praying in tongues is speaking to God

> 1 Corinthians 14:2
>
> But he who speaks in a tongue does not speak to men but to God, for no-one understands him; however, in the spirit he speaks mysteries.

Many Christians wonder whether God hears their prayers. The Word tells us that when we pray in tongues, we are speaking to God. That means when we pray in tongues, God definitely hears us.

Do not judge anyone who is praying in tongues, because they are not talking to you. They are talking to God and that should be respected.

Praying in tongues is God speaking to you

Tongues is a universal language of the Spirit and is a means whereby God and Spirit-filled believers communicate with each other.

Tongues is one of the gifts of the Holy Spirit. This is where God speaks to an individual or to a formal gathering by means of the gift of interpretation.

Believers are encouraged to practice the interpretation of their tongue in their personal time of prayer and allow God to reveal His Word to them. This is one of the ways God edifies us in our spiritual walk.

Praying in tongues builds you up

> 1 Corinthians 14:4
> He who speaks in a tongue edifies himself.

> Jude 20
> But you, beloved, building yourself up in your most holy faith, praying in the Holy Spirit.

Speaking in tongues is a wonderful benefit because it builds us up when we are down. Regardless of our present circumstances, we are empowered to rise above any despondency or discouragement.

Today many people suffer from depression, heartache and loneliness. Praying in tongues is a supernatural antidote against depression. When you speak in tongues it overcomes depression. If you feel despondent or if you feel your emotions are under attack, one of the ways to build up your emotions is when you pray in tongues.

Praying in tongues is a lifestyle

> Ephesians 5:18
> And do not be drunk with wine, in which is dissipation; but be filled continually with the Spirit.

Speaking in tongues is a lifestyle that should be practiced often. It should be present in your daily devotions and prayer. It is definitely not a once off experience but something that must be engaged in willfully and obediently every day. It should always form part of our daily prayer routine.

We must continue to walk in the Spirit by being filled continually with the Spirit and this is done by speaking in tongues as often as possible.

> 1 Corinthians 14:18
> I thank God that I speak in tongues more than all of you.

Paul was thankful that he spoke in tongues more than anyone else. This is a reference to the private form of tongues. He had a high regard for the personal benefit that people can receive through the private use of tongues.

Praying in tongues places you in God's will

> Romans 8:26 - 28
> Likewise the Spirit also helps in our weaknesses. For we do not know what we should pray as we ought, but the Spirit Himself makes intercession for us with groanings which cannot be uttered. Now He who searches the hearts knows what the mind of the Spirit is, because He makes intercession for the saints according to the will of God. And we know that all things work together for good to those who love God, to those who are called to His purpose.

The Holy Spirit knows what plans and purposes God has for your life but you do not always have a full reality of what He has for you. You may have a general idea due to personal prophecies etc., but details and time lines are secrets which are kept in the realm of God's Spirit.

When you pray in tongues, the Spirit invokes God's will for your life which is manifest in the natural in accordance with God's schedule and scheme of things.

> 1 Corinthians 14:2
> But he who speaks in a tongue does not speak to men but to God, for no-one understands him; however, in the spirit he speaks mysteries.

God is a master builder and when we pray in tongues, He builds things for us in the Spirit which are mysteries that are hidden from us. One day, as we take a corner in our faith, God surprises us with His supernatural blessings.

You do not have to make it happen because God will ensure that it happens. All you have to do is to pray in tongues.

Many people never experience this blessing because they are too hasty or they are trying to help God. God is a slow builder but what He builds in the Spirit will become a reality and a blessing and it will be His perfect will for your life.

There are treasures that are locked up in the Spirit realm that are only meant for you and the key is tongues. These are the secret plans or mysteries that are hidden from each of us. When we speak in tongues God unlocks the treasures in heaven. There are secrets that God has for every one of us individually and one of the ways of accessing those secrets is to pray in the Holy Spirit.

Speaking in tongues allows us to pray for things and situations we do not know about. There are a lot of dangerous threats to our lives that we do not know about. But praying in tongues helps us to pray for these things as well and we can trust God to step in and help us in these unknown areas. If we do not know about these things we will not know how to pray for those areas.

Praying in tongues can be done in public

> 1 Corinthians 14:22
> Therefore tongues are for a sign, not to those who believe but to unbelievers…

Tongues are a sign to the unbeliever that Jesus is alive. Do not be intimidated by the presence of unbelievers in church services. Many times, Christian leaders become embarrassed when the Holy Spirit moves and when people worship the Lord in tongues just in case other people might become offended. Many times we grieve the Holy Spirit by controlling what God wants to do in a meeting.

In fact, it is in meetings like these that people are convicted by the Holy Spirit and they give their lives to the Lord. They also have the opportunity to receive the baptism in the Holy Spirit in meetings that are anointed.

Praying with the Spirit is not a sophisticated tongue

Tongues is not a sophisticated language and believers should not practice their tongue in order for it to become mature.

Some people teach that the more you speak in tongues the more sophisticated you sound. Praying in tongues is always going to sound foolish. Some people have tried to develop their tongue but this is not Scriptural. Do not allow people to judge your tongue.

Praying with the Spirit is not gibberish

When you pray in tongues you are not speaking gibberish. Tongues are foolish to ordinary people but it is the power of God in your Christian walk. It may not sound like a language, but it is. It is a heavenly language that communicates with God.

Praying in tongues is not hypnotic

Speaking in tongues is not hypnotic and a person who is speaking in tongues or singing in tongues is not chanting.

When the Spirit of God comes on flesh, there can be fleshly or emotional outbursts. People may look like they are mesmerized, but they are not.

When you are speaking in tongues you are conscious and you know what is happening because you have not engaged your mind, but your spirit man.

Praying in tongues bypasses your mind

> 1 Corinthians 14:14
>
> For if I pray in a tongue, my spirit prays, but my mind is unfruitful.

Speaking in tongues is important for many reasons and not only the evidence that you have received the Holy Spirit. It should be a part of everyday life. It is a way to communicate directly from your heart to the Father bypassing your brain with its doubts and fears.

When we pray in tongues our spirit man engages directly with the Spirit of God. The Holy Spirit provides the words to our spirits which we then speak out of our mouths. This bypasses the mind which is not engaged in the tongue talking exercise. That is why a person can read a book or write a letter while they are speaking in tongues. They say men generally cannot do two things at the same time. However, this is now disputed!

While there are many kinds of prayers, it is wonderful to have the ability to pray in tongues without taxing the mind. The mind can rest or do something else while the spirit prays.

Praying in tongues should not be forbidden

> 1 Corinthians 14:39
> Therefore, my brothers, be eager to prophesy, and do not forbid speaking in tongues.

The final word on tongues in the entire New Testament is that speaking in tongues must not be forbidden. Christians today should be following Paul's guidelines just as they did in the first century so that they can be edified.

Praying in tongues builds up your faith

> Jude 20
> Building yourself up in your most holy faith praying in the Holy Ghost.

The Bible tells us that without faith it is impossible to please God. God blessed Abraham tremendously because he was a man of faith. By exercising his faith, Abraham came into right standing with God and he was abundantly blessed for it.

Christians sometimes struggle to exercise their faith. But praying in tongues is a supernatural way to build up your faith. Tongues builds you up in your faith and releases the hidden wisdom of God.

When your faith is down or if you feel that your faith is under attack, spend time praying in the Holy Spirit so that your faith can be built up. It will bring you in right standing with God and He will bless you.

Praying in tongues can be at any time any place

> 1 Timothy 2:8
> I desire therefore that the men pray everywhere, lifting up holy hands, without wrath and doubting.

Praying in tongues can be done anywhere and at almost any time after you are baptized in the Holy Spirit.

You can pray in tongues while travelling, while reading, while listening, etc.

Praying in tongues refreshes our spirits and our minds

> Isaiah 28:11-12
> For with stammering lips and another tongue He will speak to this people, To whom He said, "This is the rest with which You may cause the weary to rest," And, "This is the refreshing"; Yet they would not hear.

Speaking in tongues refreshes our spirits and our minds. A rest comes to those who accept the blessing of speaking in tongues. Our minds can rest while we speak in tongues and we can receive power from God through it which positively affects our physical health as well.

Praying in tongues yields the tongue to God

> James 3:8
> But no man can tame the tongue. It is an unruly evil, full of deadly poison.

We yield our tongue to God when we speak in tongues.

The tongue is by nature the most unruly member of the body and the most difficult to control.

By speaking in tongues we learn to quiet our tongues from saying wrong and hurtful things. Instead we train our tongues to speak things that are positive and life giving.

Praying in tongues places you in God's presence

> Revelation 4:1
> I was in the Spirit on the Lord's Day, and I heard behind me a loud voice, as of a trumpet. After these things I looked, and behold, a door standing open in heaven. And the first voice which I heard was like a trumpet speaking with me, saying, "Come up here, and I will show you things which must take place after this."

God lives in the realm of the Spirit. When we walk in the Spirit, we are able to translate ourselves from the natural environment into the environment of the Spirit which is the realm of God's presence.

John was banished to the isle of Patmos. In the natural, it was a very hard place to be as there was no shelter or food.

Instead of focusing on the natural and complaining to God, John engaged the Spirit realm and was taken into heaven into the presence of the Lord.

We need to walk in the Spirit and not in the flesh. One of the ways that we can walk in the Spirit is by engaging the Spirit of God through tongues. Speaking in tongues strengthens our relationship with God which will result in greater love and faith being experienced.

This results in the manifestation of the fruit of the Spirit and we can experience joy, peace, love, etc.

By living in the realm of the Spirit we can enjoy all these blessings and separate ourselves from the works of the flesh. We can escape the temptation of pride, adultery, murder, stealing etc., as they do not reside in the realm of the Spirit.

Praying in tongues is for the present day believer

> Mark 16:17;20
> And these signs will follow them that believe. In my name they will cast out demons; they shall speak with new tongues. And they went out and preached everywhere, the Lord working with them and confirming the word through the accompanying signs.

Praying in tongues is for every believer. It is God's plan and desire that every born again believer becomes filled with the Holy Spirit. There is no prerequisite to be a tongue talking believer except that you must be saved and you must be willing to yield to the Spirit of God. God is not a respecter of persons.

Paul wanted everyone to speak in tongues because it edified him when he spoke in tongues. All Christians benefit from praying with the Spirit.

> Acts 2:39
> For the promise is for you and your children and for all who are far off, as many as the Lord our God shall call to Himself.

We may be far off from the day of Pentecost but the promise of the Holy Spirit is for each and every one of us.

Praying in tongues is an evidence of God's power

> Acts 1:8
> But you shall receive power when the Holy Spirit has come upon you; and you shall be witnesses to Me in Jerusalem, and in all Judea and Samaria, and to the end of the earth.

When you are filled with the Holy Spirit you receive power. God empowers you to become an effective witness.

THE FIVE-FOLD PRAYER

Praying in tongues ensures victory in the battle

Praying with the Spirit is a powerful and effective defense against the plans and purposes of the enemy. Praying with the Spirit confuses the strategies of the enemy and helps us overcome the temptations of the world.

Praying with the Spirit is an important ongoing activity of spiritual warfare because it maintains an open dialogue with God through the Holy Spirit.

In Ephesians 6, Paul gives us detailed instructions how we can prepare our defense against the attacks of the devil. He tells us that we do not battle human enemies because it is a spiritual battle. However, these attacks always have a human face. The devil will use other people to harass and torment us. After listing all the requirements for preparation for spiritual warfare, Paul ends with this passage of Scripture which proves that it is very important to wage spiritual warfare by praying in tongues. In this case the people that the devil uses are probably unknown to us.

> Ephesians 6:18
> Praying always with all prayer and supplication in the Spirit.

The book of Jude also teaches us to pray in the Holy Spirit to combat the enemy. But this time he refers to people the devil uses that are known to us. They could either be family members or members in the Body of Christ.

We are assured of victory when we wage warfare against the plans of the enemy, whether he uses people who are known to us or whether they are unknown to us.

The devil can come against the Word in your life, he can come against your faith, he can come against your beliefs, but there is one thing that the devil cannot come against and that is the power of tongues in your life.

It is one of the things that Satan hates. That is why attacks against the church have been attacks against the Holy Spirit and against speaking in tongues because the devil knows it is one thing that hurts him.

Conclusion

God bless you as you develop a regular lifestyle of praying with the Spirit. You will begin to see God's purposes manifest in your life and every prayer supernaturally answered in the name of Jesus!

If you have not received the baptism in the Holy Spirit, ask God to fill you or ask your pastor to pray for you. Do not give up until you can speak in tongues.

Just a thought…

Tongues are the spiritual building blocks that God uses to build our Holy Ghost surprises.

CHAPTER 6

Prayer, Praise and Worship

In the early years of my ministry, I asked the Holy Spirit to give me a prayer strategy that would ensure an effective prayer life for me as an individual, for my family as well as for my ministry. After much fasting and seeking the Lord, God gave me this wonderful prayer model which I have been using for many years. It is very effective and I can confidently say that almost every request and petition that I have brought before the Lord in prayer has been answered supernaturally.

> 1 Corinthian 14:14-15
>
> For if I pray in a tongue, my spirit prays, but my understanding in unfruitful. What is the conclusion then? I will pray with the spirit, and I will pray with the understanding. I will sing with the spirit and I will also sing with the understanding.

When one studies the above passage of Scripture, it becomes evident that God wants us to spend our prayer time in four ways:

- To pray in tongues
- To pray in English (or your home language)
- To sing in tongues
- To sing in English (or your home language)

THE FIVE-FOLD PRAYER

Paul makes four choices when it comes to his prayer life by making four "I will" statements. This suggests a determination and a standard which he set for himself as an act of obedience to the Spirit of God. What a contrast to the five "I will" statements Satan made when he rebelled against God.

> Isaiah 14:13-14
>
> For you have said in your heart: 'I will ascend into heaven, I will exalt my throne above the stars of God; I will also sit on the mount of the congregation On the farthest sides of the north; I will ascend above the heights of the clouds, I will be like the Most High.'

Your prayer time can now also incorporate praise and worship.

Prayer	**Praise and Worship**
• I will pray with the Spirit • I will pray with the understanding	• I will sing with the Spirit • I will sing with the understanding

The above circle represents four equal quarters which suggest that you can divide your prayer time up in four equal time periods. For example, if you have set aside an hour for prayer use this time as follows:

- Pray with the Spirit   15 minutes
- Pray with the Understanding   15 minutes
- Sing with the Spirit   15 minutes
- Sing with the Understanding   15 minutes

I will pray with the Spirit

It is interesting to note that that one's prayer time begins first with praying in tongues. It is advisable to have all the Scriptures with you relating to praying in tongues. Prayer these passages of the Word out audibly before you start praying in tongues.

Tongues is a perfect effective prayer and produces good fruit.

THE FIVE-FOLD PRAYER

I will pray with the understanding

To pray with the understanding means you pray in a known language such as your home language. Use this opportunity to formulate prayers that conform to the Word of God.

Jesus warns us against vain repetitions when we pray. It is amazing how we repeat ourselves when we pray. I encourage believers to have their prayers written in a prayer book together with the relevant Scripture verses. It ensures that you do not run out of words after a few minutes of prayer. It also helps you to keep your prayers focused. Praying the Word is powerful because God's Word always produces something.

> Isaiah 55:11
> So shall My word be that goes forth from My mouth: it shall not return to Me void, but it shall accomplish what I please, and it shall prosper in the thing which I sent it.

Praying with the understanding or with a known language can include prayers for your country, your city, the Body of Christ, your local church, yourself, your spouse, your children, your family members, and many more.

I will sing with the Spirit

Our minds can actually come between us and God. Music can turn your mind toward God and it will deepen your relationship with Him.

Singing in tongues takes us to that secret place in the Spirit. These may not be songs that you will be able to repeat again, but are songs coming from your spirit to God. God always exhorts us through His Word to sing a new song to Him.

Throughout the Bible, there are references to God's people singing songs to Him. Spiritual songs are spontaneous songs that come from our spirit man which connects us to the Spirit of God.

Ask God to enhance your music gift and start writing songs to the Lord. These can be birthed in the Spirit when you sing in tongues. Spend a quarter of your prayer time singing in tongues. Play worship music in the background.

This is a time you can spend in praise and worship in the Spirit. Singing in tongues helps us to become filled with His Spirit because as we sing we are continually being filled with the Spirit.

I will sing with the understanding

Singing with the understanding means singing songs in a known language such as your home language. Spend a quarter of your prayer time singing. As you enter into this time of praise and worship, you can sing songs that you normally sing at church during praise and worship or you can play music in the background and sing.

Music is an important part of praise and worship. God created music. He loves all kinds of music.

David was anointed and wrote many songs of praise and worship. His desire was that the whole earth should worship and praise God.

So what is the five-fold prayer?

As I said before, many years ago the Holy Spirit to give me a prayer strategy that has enabled me to prayer effectively with 100% prayer results.

I have shared these secrets with you in this book.

It is a successful prayer model which you can start implementing immediately.

It is very effective and I can confidently say that almost every request and petition that I have brought before the Lord in prayer has been answered supernaturally.

We have seen that there are four ways to spend our time when we pray.

THE FIVE-FOLD PRAYER

Fasting is referred to as sacrificial prayer and is a vital component of our prayer life.

In order to prayer effectively and expect 100% results from your prayer life, make sure you implement this five-fold prayer model.

1. Praying in tongues
2. Praying in your home language
3. Singing in tongues
4. Singing in your home language
5. Fasting

Just a thought…

Do you want every one of your prayers answered? We all do. Effective prayer ensures answers to each and every one of our prayers and begins with implementing this five-fold prayer model. Implement this prayer plan and see how your life will change over the next couple of years. Remember - increasing your <u>prayer life</u> increases your <u>success life.</u>

CHAPTER 7

Examples of a Prayer Book

Make sure you have a prayer book with you when you pray. Include passages from the Word which you can declare over your life. Take your Bible with you when you pray because God will remind you of Scriptures during your prayer time so that He can encourage you or instruct you.

Also take your prophecies with you and pray them out loud because they represent your future and God's will for your life.

Always make sure you can retreat to a secure place where you will not be disturbed and where you can pray and worship God out loud. Play music in the background especially when you are praying in tongues or when you are singing either in tongues or in your home language.

God bless you as you implement these suggestions by faith. Email me any testimonies you may have by using this prayer model: dean@tiuniversity.com

I have included an example of my prayer book in this chapter.

THE FIVE-FOLD PRAYER

Opening prayer

Father I come to you in the mighty name of Jesus. I declare that my prayers are not repetitive but are effective, producing that for which it has been sent.

There are things that I know and things that I do not know, that are hidden in You and can only be accessed by Your Spirit. I pray that You will reveal all the hidden plans and purposes that You have for my life.

I declare that my prayer is effective and fervent and avails much and that I avoid vain repetitions. My prayer life consists of praying with the Spirit, praying with the understanding, singing with the Spirit, singing with the understanding and fasting.

The Word of the Lord is tested and tried - Your Word has revived me and given me life. Forever, O Lord, Your Word is settled in heaven. Your Word is a lamp unto my feet and a light unto my path.

Let my prayer be set forth as incense before You, the lifting up of my hands as the evening sacrifice. Blessed be the Lord God who daily loads us with His benefits. Father your mercies are new every morning. Lord, I declare that any need that may present itself this day will be supplied by You supernaturally.

Father Yours is the greatness, the power and the glory, the victory and the majesty, for all that is in heaven and in earth is Yours. You are exalted as Head over all.

EXAMPLES OF A PRAYER BOOK

Father I now pray in tongues

1 Corinthians 14:14 - 15

For if I pray in a tongue, my spirit prays, but my understanding is unfruitful. What is the conclusion then? I will pray with the spirit, and I will pray with the understanding. I will sing with the spirit and I will also sing with the understanding.

1 Corinthians 14:2

But he who speaks in a tongue does not speak to men but to God, for no-one understands him; however, in the spirit he speaks mysteries.

1 Corinthians 14:4

He who speaks in a tongue edifies himself.

Jude 20

But you, beloved, building yourself up on your most holy faith, praying in the Holy Spirit.

Romans 8:26 - 28

Likewise the Spirit also helps in our weaknesses. For we do not know what we should pray as we ought, but the Spirit Himself makes intercession for us with groanings which cannot be uttered. Now He who searches the hearts knows what the mind of the Spirit is, because He makes intercession for the saints according to the will of God. And we know that all things work together for good to those who love God, to those who are called to His purpose.

Mark 16 :17

And these signs will follow them that believe. In my name they will cast out demons; they shall speak with new tongues.

Ephesians 6:18

Praying always with all prayer and supplication in the Spirit...

EXAMPLES OF A PRAYER BOOK

Father I now pray with my understanding

Father I come to you in the name of Jesus. I pray Your Word because You have said that Your Word will not return unto You void.

> Isaiah 55:11
>
> So shall My word be that goes forth from My mouth: it shall not return to Me void, but it shall accomplish what I please, and it shall prosper in the thing which I sent it.

> Hebrews 4:12
>
> For the word of God is living and powerful and sharper than any two-edged sword, piercing even to the division of soul and spirit, and of joints and marrow, and is a discerner of the thoughts and intents of the heart.

> Joshua 1:8
>
> This Book of the Law shall not depart from your mouth, but you shall meditate in it day and night, that you may

observe to do according to all that is written in it. For then you shall make your way prosperous, and then you will have good success

a. I pray for my country

1 Timothy 2:1-4

Therefore I exhort first of all that supplications, prayers, intercessions, and giving of thanks be made for all men, for kings and all who are in authority, that we may lead a quiet and peaceable life in all godliness and reverence. For this is good and acceptable in the sight of God our Saviour, who desires all men to be saved and come to the knowledge of truth.

2 Chronicles 7:14

If my people who are called by my name, shall humble themselves and pray, and seek my face, and turn from their wicked ways; then I will hear from heaven, and will forgive their sin, and will heal their land.

I pray for our President and all the politicians in Government. I pray Lord that you will surround them with godly men and women of Kingdom insight who will advise them in the ways of the Lord.

I pray for peace to continue in this land and that racial harmony will persist. I pray that the economy in our country will strengthen mightily.

Father I thank you that our land is free from any aggression that may cause destruction to the economy and confidence in the country.

I thank you for the freedom we have to exercise our faith without hindrance from the authorities. Father let us use this freedom to advance Your Kingdom in every way, be it by word, literature or the media.

I thank you for the revival which is coming to this land, for Your Word tells me that in the last days, You will pour out Your Spirit upon all flesh and that our sons and daughters shall prophesy; the young shall see visions and the old shall dream dreams.

b. I pray for my city

> Isaiah 62:6-7
>
> I have set watchmen upon your walls, O Jerusalem; they shall never hold their peace day or night. You who make mention of the Lord, do not keep silent, and give Him no rest till He establishes and till He makes Jerusalem a praise on the earth.

Father I thank you for the city where you have planted me. I have been empowered by Your Spirit to be a witness in this city and even to the ends of the earth.

I thank you for the peace and stability that prevails in this city. I come against all the demonic strongholds that hold this city in bondage to the evil one.

I pray that Your Word will bring light to the city in which I live and that our community will be transformed by the Gospel of Jesus Christ.

c. I pray for the Body of Christ

Father I pray that the church of Jesus Christ will increase in the knowledge of You and may walk worthy and fully pleasing to You and will be equipped by the Word.

No weapon formed against Your church will prosper and no tongue that is raised shall stand. You have defeated the devil and have put all principalities and powers under Your feet. You have given us Your name which is above every other name. At the name of Jesus, every knee shall bow and every tongue confess that Jesus Christ is Lord.

> Matthew 16:18
> …I will build My church, and the gates of Hades shall not prevail against it.

I thank You for the apostles, prophets, evangelists, pastors and teachers, who are given for the perfecting of the saints, for the work of the ministry, for the edifying of the body of Christ till we all come in the unity of the faith and of the knowledge of the Son of God to a perfect man and to the measure of the stature of the fullness of Christ.

Jesus, You love the church, You gave your life for the church and redeemed it by Your blood. We are one Body and one Head, one Spirit, one Lord, one faith, one baptism, one God and Father of all. I thank you that the whole body is knit together in covenant one with the other.

> Ephesians 3:21
> Unto Him be glory in the Church by Christ Jesus throughout all ages, world without end. Amen.

d. I pray for my local church

Father in the name of Jesus, I come into Your presence thanking You for my local church which has been birthed by your Spirit. The ministry operates in excellence and has ministry gifts for the edifying of the local church and will be used to birth revival in our local area and to all nations.

I ask for the wisdom of God in meeting every need. I thank you for the facilities which we have that will more than meet every need. Our church is prospering financially and we have more than enough to meet the financial needs relative to our vision. We have everything we need to bring the Gospel of Jesus to every home in our area and to all nations.

THE FIVE-FOLD PRAYER

We are a praying church praying always with all prayer and supplication in the Spirit, being watchful to this end with all perseverance for all the saints. We call those things that be not as though they were and wage good warfare according to the prophecies concerning our local church.

We have written the vision and made it plain on tablets so that we may run with it for the vision is for an appointed time. We wait for it for it shall surely come. It will not tarry. We confess that in blessing You bless us and in multiplying you multiply our seed as the stars of heaven and as the sand which is upon the sea shore. Our seed shall possess the gate of our enemies and in our seed shall all the nations of the earth be blessed, because we have obeyed Your voice. Fill every vacant place in our local church.

Father I come to you in the name of Jesus and intercede on behalf of every member of our church. I thank you that we all speak the same thing and that there is no division among us. We are perfectly joined together in the same mind and are at all times in one accord.

I pray for all the Pastors, Heads of Departments, Bible School, Children's church, Youth, Music Ministry, Intercession and ministry teams.

Thank you that the members are no longer children tossed to and fro and carried about with every wind of doctrine, by the trickery of men, in the cunning craftiness of deceitful plotting, but speak the truth in love and grow up in all things into

Christ, from whom the whole body are joined and knit together, edifying itself in love.

Thank You that the members put off concerning their former conduct and are renewed in the spirit of their minds and that each one speaks the truth with each other. I thank You Father that no corrupt word proceeds from their mouths, but what is good for edification, imparting grace to others, being kind to one another and forgiving one another.

I thank you that they will apply your Word and will develop a breakthrough mentality and that prosperity and success will be manifest in their lives. May they prosper as their souls prosper. I thank You Lord that the members meet the needs of others and I ask for the wisdom of God in meeting these needs. I thank You that they take heed to the ministry to which You have called them. I thank You Lord that they will not neglect the assembling of themselves together, especially as we see that Day approaching.

Lord, Your Word declares, that all glory and honor is due to You. I give You honor, glory, and thanks, for the following:

- Freedom from internal strife, sin and division
- The numerical growth that is taking place
- The finances which are coming in

THE FIVE-FOLD PRAYER

I pray that the lives of our people will be changed supernaturally and that they continue to grow from level to level, from glory to glory.

> Galatians 4:19
> ... until Christ is formed in you.

I thank you Lord, that You are able to do exceedingly, abundantly, above all that we can ask or think, according to the power that is working in us.

Father I come to You in the name of Jesus and present all our services before You. I pray that the people who hear Your Word will not be able to resist the wisdom and the inspiration of the Holy Spirit that will be imparted. As Your Word comes forth, I pray for an anointing of the Holy Spirit that will cause people to open their spiritual eyes and ears and turn from darkness to light and from the power of Satan to You.

I commit all our meetings to You. Thank you for the unsaved people that You will send to the meetings so that they can give their lives to you. Thank You for those that will come who have a spiritual need so that they can experience Your miracle working power and love for them. I confess that Your Word will transform the people and cause them to realize that they are joint heirs with Jesus. I believe that every need of every person will be met spiritually, physically, mentally and financially. I declare that our numbers will increase more and more week after week.

e. I pray for myself

Father I come to you in the name of Jesus and present myself before you. You have formed my inward parts and You covered me in my mother's womb. I praise You for I am fearfully and wonderfully made.

My frame was not hidden from You when I was made in secret and skillfully wrought in the lowest parts of the earth. You saw my substance yet unformed and in Your Book you determined beforehand all my days. I thank you for all the prophetic words which have been spoken over my life and I pray them into manifestation. You have begun a good work in me and You are faithful to complete it. I do not have any fear or anxiety because You have given me a spirit of power and of a sound mind.

I do not neglect meeting with my fellow brothers and sisters in Christ. I am redeemed from the curse, because Jesus bore my sicknesses and carried my diseases in His own body. By His stripes I am healed. I forbid any sickness or disease to operate in my body. I honor You in my body.

I have the mind of Christ. I am a believer and not a doubter. I am the head and not the tail and I succeed in every aspect of my life. I am an overcomer, more than a conqueror through Jesus. I am a useful member in my local church. I am created in Christ Jesus for good works. Your Word dwells richly in me.

> 1 John 4:17
> As He is so are we in this world.

I pray Lord that you will not lead me into temptation, but that You will deliver me from evil.

> 1 Corinthians 10:13
>
> There has no temptation taken you but such as is common to man: but God is faithful, who will not allow you to be tempted above that which you are able; but will with the temptation also make a way to escape, that you may be able to bear it.

Lord, forgive all my sins as I forgive others who have sinned against me. I declare that I have no bitterness in my heart toward anyone.

I now pray the prayer of Jabez over my life.

> 1 Chronicles 4:10
>
> And Jabez called on the God of Israel saying, "Oh that You would bless me indeed, and enlarge my territory, that Your hand would be with me, and that You would keep me from evil, that I may not cause pain!" So God granted him what he requested.

f. I pray for my marriage

> Ephesians 5:21-31
>
> Submitting to one another in the fear of God.
>
> Wives, submit to your own husbands, as to the Lord. For the husband is the head of the wife, even as Christ is the head of the church: and He is the Savior of the body.

Therefore, just as the church is subject to Christ, so let the wives be to their own husbands in everything.

Husbands, love your wives, just as Christ also loved the church, and gave Himself for her, that He might sanctify and cleanse her with the washing of water by the word, that He might present her to Himself a glorious church, not having spot or wrinkle or any such thing; but that she should be holy and without blemish.

So husbands ought to love their own wives as their own bodies; he who loves his wife loves himself. For no one ever hated his own flesh; but nourishes and cherishes it, just as the Lord does the church. For we are members of His body, of His flesh, and of His bones.

For this cause a man shall leave his father and mother and be joined to his wife, and the two shall become one flesh.

This is a great mystery: but I speak concerning Christ and the church. Nevertheless let each one of you in particular so love his own wife as himself; and let the wife see that she respects her husband.

Matthew 19:6

So then, they are longer two but one flesh. Therefore what God has joined together, let not man separate.

Father we are submitted to one another in love. I thank You that we are a couple whose marriage is an example to others and that we are successful in everything we do.

The Lord commands a blessing upon our house and in all to which we set our hands He will bless us in this land.

We are anxious for nothing because you protect our marriage as well as all our possessions. No physical harm comes to us. We live in health and healing and are promised a long fruitful life. Together we will fulfill our destiny in accordance with Your plan.

We live and conduct ourselves and our marriage honorably. We commit ourselves to live in mutual love and peace being of the same mind and united in spirit. Our marriage grows stronger each day in the bond of unity because it is founded on Your Word.

g. I pray for my family

> Acts 16:31
> And they said, Believe on the Lord Jesus Christ and you shall be saved, and your household.

Father I come to You in the name of Jesus concerning the members of my family.

Firstly, I pray for the members of my family who are not saved. Jesus, you have come to give life and life more abundantly, eternal life to all those who accept you as Lord and Savior and who confess with their mouth the Lord Jesus.

You are not willing that any should perish but that all my unsaved family members should come to the knowledge of the truth. I pray that you will place the right persons in their paths who will share Your Gospel in a special way that will cause them to listen and to understand so that they will willingly surrender their lives to Jesus.

Your Word declares that You will deliver those for whom we intercede. I commit this matter into Your hands with my faith and I see each and every member of my family saved, filled with Your Spirit, with a full understanding and knowledge of Your Word. I thank You for their salvation and I rejoice for the victory.

Father I now pray for my family members who are saved. I pray that each one of them will fulfill their purpose and will walk in Your perfect will. You have begun a good work in them and will be faithful to complete it until Jesus returns. I pray that their love may abound more and more and that they will be pure and untainted and blameless and that they will serve You faithfully.

I pray that You will sanctify them completely and may their whole spirit soul and body be preserved blameless at the coming of our Lord Jesus Christ.

Father I confess Your Word over my children and apply the blood of Jesus over them for their protection. I train them up in the way that they should go and I declare that they will never depart from it.

They are disciples of Jesus and are obedient to Your will. They increase in wisdom and stature and in favor of God and man. They honor their parents, for this is the first commandment with a promise. All may be well with them and that they may live long on this earth.

As parents we will not provoke them to anger nor discourage them but will bring them up in the fear of the Lord. May we increase more and more together with our children.

h. Father I make my requests known to You

Mark 11:23

For assuredly, I say to you, whoever says to this mountain, "Be removed and be cast into the sea," and does not doubt in his heart, but believes those things he says will be done, he will have whatever he says.

Philippians 4:19

And my God shall supply all your need according to His riches in Glory by Christ Jesus.

2 Peter 3:9

The Lord is not slack concerning His promise, as some count slackness, but is longsuffering toward us, not willing that any should perish but that all should come to repentance.

EXAMPLES OF A PRAYER BOOK

Date	Request	Date Answered

THE FIVE-FOLD PRAYER

Father I now sing with the Spirit

Spend one quarter of your time singing with the Spirit as you praise and worship God with the Spirit.

Father I now sing with the understanding

Spend one quarter of your time singing in your home language as you praise and worship God with the Spirit.

CHAPTER 8

Prayer References from the Word

Use these Scripture verses to build Word-based prayers for any situation you may be facing.

To pray for your country

    1 Timothy 2:1 - 4
    Psalm 105:14
    Proverbs 2:10 - 15
    Proverbs 2:21 - 22
    Proverbs 20:26 & 28
    Proverbs 21:1
    Proverbs 16:10 & 12 & 13
    Proverbs 28:2
    Proverbs 29:2
    Acts 12:24
    Psalm 68:11

To pray for your city

    Acts 1:18
    Luke 23:34

THE FIVE-FOLD PRAYER

Hebrews 4:16
2 Corinthians S 4:4
Psalm 147:15
Ephesians 6:12
Acts 12:24
Psalm 101:8
Jeremiah 29:7 - 8
John 16:8
Psalm 29:7 – 8
Jeremiah 29:11
Psalm 55:9
Proverbs 11:11
Ephesians 2:2
Acts 26:18

To pray for the church

Colossians 1:9 - 14
Colossians 3:12 - 17
Colossians 2:5 - 7
1 Timothy 1:18
Acts 4:24
Ephesians 4:11 - 13
Romans 4:17
Acts 2:1 - 2
1 Corinthians 1:10
Genesis 22:17 - 18
Acts 4:29

Habakkuk 2:2 - 3
Ephesians 4:11 - 15
Philippians 4:19
Romans 5:5
Psalm 63:4
Exodus 35:33

To pray for others

Colossians 4:17
Acts 13:36
Luke 2:52
Colossians 4:12
Galatians 4:9
Romans 15:5 - 6
Psalm 25:4 - 7
Ephesians 1:17 - 19
Ephesians 3:16 - 21

To pray for yourself

1 Timothy 1:18
Philippians 4:6
Psalm 139:13 - 18
Galatians 3:13
2 Corinthians 10:18
Matthew 8:17
Philippians 2:9 - 11

THE FIVE-FOLD PRAYER

1 Peter 2:24
Philippians 4:13
1 Corinthians 2:16
Philippians 4:19
Hebrews 4:14
Hebrews 11:6
Romans 10:17
Hebrews 12:2
1 John 4:16
Romans 5:5
1 John 5:18
Galatians 1:4
Ephesians 2:6
2 Timothy 1:17
Romans 8:31
1 John 5:4 - 5
Ephesians 2:10
Philippians 2:13
Colossians 3:16
Philippians 1:6

To pray for your marriage (where applicable)

Matthew 19:5 - 6
John 16:23 - 24
Philippians 4:6
2 Peter 3:9
Deuteronomy 28:5 & 8

PRAYER REFERENCES FROM THE WORD

To pray for your children (where applicable)

Luke 2:52
Ephesians 1:16 - 23
Psalm 115:14

To pray for your family members

1 Thessalonians 5:23 - 24
Philippians 1:6
Matthew 15:4

To walk in love and forgiveness

Romans 5:5
Philippians 1:9-11
1 John 2:5
John 13:34
1 John 4:18
1 Corinthians 3:6
Daniel 1:9
1 Corinthians 13:4-8
Romans 12:14
Ephesians 3:17
Matthew 5:44
Romans 8:31,39
Romans 12:16-18
Mark 11:25

THE FIVE-FOLD PRAYER

Romans 12:10
Ephesians 4:32
Philippians 2:2
1 Peter 3:8,11,12
Ephesians 4:31
Colossians 1:10
Ephesians 4:27
Romans 5:5
John 1:9
Philippians 1:9,11

To live in victory in every situation

Colossians 1:13
Hebrews 12:1,2
Romans 8:2
2 Timothy 1:12
1 Peter 5:6,7
Philippians 4:8
Psalm 55:22
John 14:1
Psalm 138:8
James 1:22-25
Philippians 4:6
2 Corinthians 10:5
Isaiah 55:11
Psalm 91:10
1 Peter 2:24

Psalm 34:7
Matthew 8:17
2 Timothy 1:7
Galatians 3:13
Hebrews 4:12,14
James 4:7
Proverbs 4:22
Ephesians 6:12
Romans 8:2
2 Corinthians 10:4
Ephesians 6:11,16
Psalm 91:1
Psalm 112:7
Psalm 9:9-10
Ephesians 4:27
Psalm 42:5,11
Luke 4:18,19
Psalm 146:8
2 Timothy 1:7
Psalm 31:22-24
1 Corinthians 2:16
Isaiah 35:3,4
Philippians 2:5
Isaiah 54:14
Ephesians 4:23,24
Isaiah 50:10
Hebrews 12:12,13
Jeremiah 29:11-13

THE FIVE-FOLD PRAYER

Isaiah 60:1
Isaiah 26:3
Galatians 1:4
John 14:27
Nehemiah 8:10
James 4:7
Romans 10:9,10,13
Hebrews 4:14-16
Matthew 18:18,19
1 John 4:4
Romans 8:4,9
1 Corinthians 6:12
Romans 12:21
2 Corinthians 10:4,5
Ephesians 3:16
Romans 13:14
Ephesians 6:10-17

Books by Dr. Jeff van Wyk

1. *The Five-Fold Anointing*
2. *Learning to Lead in Ministry*
3. *Christian Ethics*
4. *World Religions*
5. *Principles of Financial Freedom*
6. *The Five-Fold Prayer*
7. *Spiritual Battlefields*
8. *The Prophetic Anointing*

Dr. Jeff van Wyk is the Senior Pastor of Joy Ministries in Germiston, South Africa. He is also the President of Team Impact University, USA.

Contact Details:

PO Box 15611
Lambton
1411
South Africa

+ 27 11 834 0735

jeff@joyministries.co.za

www.joyministries.com
www.tiuniversity.com
www.jeffvanwyk.com

Ecclesiastes 12:12

And further, my son, be admonished by these. Of making many books *there is* no end, and much study *is* wearisome to the flesh.

Whether you are searching for a Bible College, Christian University, Theological Seminary or Christian College – you have come to the right place! Team Impact University is an accredited online Christian learning facility that caters for all levels of anointed Christian study.

www.tiuniversity.com